AN ADVENTURE IN DISCIPLESHIP

AN ADVENTURE
IN DISCIPLESHIP

THE SERVANTS OF
CHRIST THE KING

ROGER LLOYD

With a preface by
the Bishop of Ely

LONGMANS, GREEN AND CO
LONDON · NEW YORK · TORONTO

LONGMANS, GREEN AND CO LTD
6 & 7 CLIFFORD STREET LONDON W I
BOSTON HOUSE STRAND STREET CAPE TOWN
531 LITTLE COLLINS STREET MELBOURNE

LONGMANS, GREEN AND CO INC
55 FIFTH AVENUE NEW YORK 3

LONGMANS, GREEN AND CO
20 CRANFIELD ROAD TORONTO 16

ORIENT LONGMANS LTD
CALCUTTA BOMBAY MADRAS
DELHI VIJAYAWADA DACCA

First published 1953
Third Impression 1955

PRINTED IN GREAT BRITAIN BY
NORTHUMBERLAND PRESS LIMITED
GATESHEAD ON TYNE

PREFACE BY THE BISHOP OF ELY

SHORTLY after I came to Ely, I received, with other Bishops, a letter telling me about the proposal to form what is now called "The Servants of Christ the King." I had already been increasingly impatient at being forced to spend much time on organization, committees and meetings (necessary, alas, as are some of them) and this came as a breath of fresh air. I said so: and before I knew where I was, I had been asked by the Archbishops to become Visitor. Thus in a very insignificant way I have had a part in one of the positive evangelistic efforts of the Anglican Church to-day.

What you will read is a story of sincere effort, made by ordinary lay people who have learnt to love our Lord, to serve Him and to tell others about Him. It is a story of effort—not of success, though at times God has granted it. You will read of failures and mistakes also. S.C.K. does not want publicity: indeed this book has been written only after many heart-searchings and criticisms; but its members believe that under God they have been enabled to do a tiny bit to help forward His Kingdom, and perhaps some who read will be called to join with them in the work.

✠EDWARD ELY.

Quinquagesima, 1953.

CONTENTS

Chapter One

THE COMMISSIONING OF THIS BOOK

THERE was nothing in the least solemn or portentous about the ten people who were sitting on that swelteringly hot afternoon in May 1952 round the table of a committee room in Church House, Westminster. Neither their appearance which was quite unremarkable, nor their bearing which was exceedingly cheerful, gave any obvious impression of the great importance of what they were trying to do, though they themselves had no doubt whatever about that. The society or fellowship or movement—it is all three in one—to which they belonged and for which they had been called to take counsel, had always discouraged much solemnity and forbidden pompousness, and they were all well used to its ways and schooled in its values. They were about the King's business. This King was Christ, and His business and theirs was the establishment of His Kingdom. It was no small or parochial matter for ten ordinary people to be trafficking with, but that in itself was all the more a reason for the cheerfulness with which they addressed themselves to it.

There would be no point in giving all their names, for only to quite small circles were most of them known. One was a mistress in a Bristol school and another was an inspector of factories from Bradford. There was a

young teacher from a High School in Portsmouth, and
the wife of the Headmaster of a Public School in the
Midlands. Next to her sat a London man who is the
secretary of a professional engineering institution, and
beyond him was a private secretary from Winchester.
Then there was a woman from Dorset who was a house-
wife and the general prop and support of her village,
which meant that of all the people present she probably
worked the hardest. Three clergymen completed the
company, over the lay members of which they were
given no special pre-eminence and desired none. Two
of them were parish priests, vicars respectively of a large
industrial town in East Anglia, and of one of the cotton
weaving towns in Lancashire, while the third was one
of the residentiary canons of a great south-country
cathedral. Their homes and work scattered them widely
and made of them outposts easily in geographical
touch with most of the country, and the range of their
experiences, occupations, and ages made of them as
fairly complete a cross-section of the Church of England
as ten people could ever claim to be.

They had gathered together the previous evening, and
that morning, after Communion in a chapel of Westminster Abbey, they addressed themselves to their work.
But they did it in their own way which was markedly
different from the way of most committees. The first
thing to be done was to keep in the chapel a corporate
half-hour's vigil of silent prayer, with no word spoken,
for "Pray first, discuss afterwards" was one of their
fundamental principles. Then each one in turn opened
his full mind on the subject concerned, and while he
spoke no one might interrupt him. When all the con-

tributions had thus been laid out on the table in full view, it became the job of general discussion to reject some, accept others, and weave these into a synthesis; and this, eventually, had to be accepted unanimously or else not accepted at all. A minority of only one would have been quite enough to disqualify the conclusions agreed to by all the others. Thus they waited upon God. It was the method, the heart, and the soul of their corporate response to Him both in action and in contemplation. It made what they did and what they were. In this way they reached all their decisions, and one of them was that this book should be written, a charge they laid upon the author, which by reason of his own promise of obedience to unanimous decisions, he was bound to accept, and is now discharging.

For he and they and some hundreds of other members of the Anglican Church up and down the country all belonged to the fellowship of a ten-year-old experiment called THE SERVANTS OF CHRIST THE KING. The heart of it is the gathering and welding together of very small communities or "cells" which, held in constant fellowship with all the others, and by the power of a common discipline, try to throw the full weight of their togetherness in Christ into the adventure of claiming all the "Kingdoms of this world" which they can reach to become the "Kingdoms of our Lord and of His Christ." These ten people were those chosen to take counsel for the whole body, and sternly forbidden to become anything remotely approaching a committee. Instead they must themselves be another S.C.K. company—the Central Company—with its own fellowship and discipline, and having as what the Quakers would call its Common Concern the care of the whole body. So a task laid on any one of its members by the unanimous call of the whole company automatically became a matter of obligation, involving obedience.

So much for the author's credentials, on which there is no need to say more. But it may be necessary to say a little by way of preface on the credentials of THE SERVANTS OF CHRIST THE KING as a whole to commission a book to be written about the fellowship, and to cause it to be written now rather than at any previous moment in the ten years of its history. The conversation round that table gave the real answer to the implied question. Here were ten people fresh from the pleasant labour of visiting each one of the different and very various S.C.K. companies in his or her own area. Experiences were told. Assessments of particular needs were made. It was clear that more was being done towards the casting down of godless strongholds than anyone outside S.C.K. had any idea of. In this place a previously very depraved person had been won for Christ. In that vigorous siege was being laid to a vast housing estate. Here the Church had a cell—an S.C.K. company —at work in a mission hospital abroad. There a young and rather brilliant secular agnostic had been gradually brought to the point where he was about to be ordained. And for all this, and far more besides, a particular method and shape of the togetherness of Christian mediocrities, not of saints, seemed incontestably to be responsible. It all added up to the discovery of a form and type of discipleship which generated power—

exactly the sort of power which the present situation most needs and so seldom gets, a modern form of the sort of power which animated the Christians of the early Church, and was the historic secret of their astounding success. The tales told so quietly that afternoon made cumulative and irresistible evidence that at least some part of the answer to the modern situation which all Christians agree in deploring had been found.

And of all that the Church as a whole knew almost nothing at all. It did not know because it had never been told. This concealment (for it really amounted to that) had been a matter of deliberate policy. From the beginning "No Publicity" had been the rule, and along the top of every S.C.K. document the words "Not for Publication" had been printed in heavy black type. No one was allowed to write articles in the Church papers to say how excellent an experiment this was. Any canvassing for recruits was no less strictly forbidden. No "organizing secretary" was allowed to stump the country "getting companies started." The whole enterprise was to be a handmaid of the Church, working in hidden anonymity under the surface of the Church's life. This was right and wise for so long as we were all groping to find our way and feeling our feet. But in practice this ideal of hidden-ness, which could never be absolute, had become less and less possible; and the attempt to maintain it had become more and more embarrassing. The time had come, judged these ten people who were in a position to know all the facts, when the old policy of No Publicity must be changed to a policy of Controlled Publicity. "If we have any part of the answer we have no right any longer to keep it to ourselves, and we ought now to tell people about it." Such was their deliberate conclusion, arrived at in conditions and under safeguards which make the use of the biblical phrase, "It seemed good to the Holy Ghost and to us" not wholly extravagant.

Such, then, is the genesis of this account of the purpose, the formation, and the history of this Anglican Society, THE SERVANTS OF CHRIST THE KING. From the beginning the whole conception was rooted in a theology. It was even more an attempt to find a body to clothe a theology than it was to produce a remedy to meet a need. Therefore the theology behind it must be defined before the history is narrated. The history, when it comes to be told, will be by no means wholly a success story. Success is there certainly, but almost as much failure. There may be an unshaken confidence among us all in the deep principles, but there is just as much fumbling, groping, and stumbling in mire and clay in the attempts to fit practical shape to the principles and express them in action for the Kingdom of God. But in spite of all that, the thing exists, and has existed for ten years, and shows no sign whatever of coming to the point where its life flags and it ought to die. Constant disappointments seem never to impair its vitality or our faith. The vision we had in 1943 we have still. Our hopes then are our hopes now. Our original belief that it is along this road or some development of it which enshrines precisely these principles. that the Church must march to win its twentieth-century kingdom is still our belief. We have seen it all happen on a very little scale, and we know beyond all peradventure that it can happen on a much larger scale.

So will you, good reader, let us tell you about it all, and share our hope, and, in due course if it seems good to you, our fellowship?

Chapter Two

THE ROOTS IN THE BIBLICAL GROUND

THE whole conception of S.C.K., it has been said, was to find a body capable of expressing a theology, and though from the first we all had our eyes fixed upon the general evangelistic need of the time it did not seem likely that it would differ in essentials from the same need as it appears in all the moments of history. The need might indeed be more obviously urgent in the twentieth than in say the twelfth century, but if it was the same need, then it would be met by the application of the same universal biblical principles. Particularly would this be so if, as we all believed, the Bible is the "Living Word of the Living God Who has Spoken," and if it was also true, as is constantly asserted, that our generation lives closer than most to the experience of biblical times. On all these grounds we had first to be sure about the theology, and only then could we go on to discuss what kind of a body in modern conditions this theology implied.

Nevertheless for the sake of convenience and clarity it will be best to be momentarily illogical and say first what S.C.K. is, and then go on to state the theological presuppositions of it. S.C.K., then, is a part of the general Cell Movement which has become such a feature of the life of the whole Church in the twentieth century. But its cells, or companies as we prefer to call them, are of a special and particular kind, and contain a combination of features not found in the Cell Movement as a whole. An S.C.K. company contains not less than three or more than twelve members, all of whom must be communicants of the Anglican Church. Nobody can be an individual member, but only a member of one of the companies, none of which can come into existence until the bishop of the diocese has given his consent. Each of these companies must be obedient to a rule of life voluntarily agreed amongst themselves, and each of them must have a priest to be its adviser, though he himself is not a member of the company. There can also be companies of priests, but they, too, must have a separate priest to advise them. All major decisions whether of the single company or of the whole body must be arrived at by a particular way of waiting upon God, which will be fully described in its place in this book, and no decisions have any force or compulsion until they are matters of free and unanimous agreement. Finally, all the companies are held together in a single and common fellowship by a whole series of devices, so that each one knows something about all the others, and the needs, the weaknesses, and the strengths of all are known to the warden and the secretary, so that pastoral care can be given to each one of them, which is just as necessary for a group of people as for each one of its individual members.

Such are the very bare bones of the skeleton of S.C.K., and at a later stage of this account they will be clothed with flesh. But the skeleton itself was born of a theology and tries to express its basic principles. We did not produce the thing first and hunt for the theology

B

afterwards. It was from the first embedded in biblical principles, and to these we now turn.

The first condition upon which alone the pagan kingdoms of this world can be brought under the divine obedience is the filling of the members of the Church with spiritual power. Since they cannot fill themselves with this grace, their first need is to yield to the inspiration of God. In practice this means that we have to create the mould or shape of association upon which the inspiration of God can come, the state of affairs on which God can get a purchase and through which He can act. The Bible makes it absolutely clear what this shape is. Hundreds of years of history may separate its writers, and their motives and methods of writing are often quite different from each other. Yet when they come to defining the conditions of divine inspiration in the world, they all say exactly the same things. Their unanimity of testimony is absolute and most impressive.

Broadly speaking they say two basic things: first, God is energy as well as love, or, as Archbishop William Temple used so often to say, Absolute Power held in control by Absolute Love; second, that it is upon the togetherness of the communities of those who love Him that His strengthening inspiration normally comes.

From Genesis to Revelation the biblical writers are sure that God is energy, that He is always intensely active, and that He immerses Himself in history from His primary act of creation onwards to the end of historic time. He works out His own purpose in the world, constantly intervening in the course of history to do so. He is always coming out of the Everywhere into the Here and out of the Eternal into the Now. The heart of this basic biblical insight into the mind and character of God is put perhaps most briefly and completely in a verse in Psalm 74, "The help that is done upon earth, God doeth it himself." Thus the initiative which was His at the moment of creation is His always, and our human initiative and energy must at all points depend on, and be linked to His own. All right action by His creatures in the world derives from His own action. It follows that the first action required of Christian people who care for the growth of the Kingdom of God is really the fostering of an attitude of mind towards God. They must yield and wait. They must be filled with expectancy. They must be still and know that because God is God He will be exalted in the world. Their first purpose must be to empty themselves that they may be filled. Their first obligation is to listen, not to act. Their first prayer must be, "Lord, teach me that I may be usable, and then use me as, where, and when seems good to Thee."

The second principle on which the biblical writers insist is that this attitude of mind which stakes all on the initiating energy of God is only fully fruitful when the mind which holds it is deliberately laid alongside other minds which are thinking in the same way. It is no doubt much that each one of us should yield separately, indeed, it is essential since no one can yield for another, but individual submission is only completed when it is made in company with others. In the Bible God's plan of redemption requires a dedicated community to be its instrument. No other authors of the ancient world are so consistently sure that it is only in the togetherness of spiritual community that we can be fully shown the things that belong to our health, and to the world's health. So the Lord in His energy and by right of His initiative is constantly shown as taking steps to create such communities. The same divine initiative which creates the world calls out Abraham and Moses, creates a nation to bear God's name, gives the Law, speaks through judges and prophets, becomes man in Christ, creates the Church, and dwells within it in inspiration through the Holy Spirit. At every point the purpose of such divine interventions is to make possible the birth and the training of a corporate body of worshippers through which His action can, so to say, become permanent. From end to end the teaching of the Bible seems to be that divine inspiration normally descends on the dedicated community, and upon specially gifted and heroic individuals in and through their membership of it. Significantly, no other sacred writings are quite so full of individual heroes who are richly and variously themselves. In a word it seems incontestably part of the divine plan that God's people should respond to Him first of all, and that they should do this together. When they do this, they will find that their separate individualities, so far from being blurred, are in fact enhanced and intensified.

Christ took over this double insight of the sacred writings of His nation, and in speech and action He endorsed them at every point. He chose twelve men out of the whole body of His first disciples. They were to be given a special training, and it chiefly consisted in learning to live together with Him. They must share a common life, experience the joy and bear the strains of being constantly together, and learn little by little that their strength together, the product of Grace, would be greater by far than the sum of their strengths in isolation, the product of nature. As this group contained in Matthew what we should nowadays call a collaborator and in Simon the Zealot a Resistance Leader, and this in a country under enemy occupation, it cannot have been easy. The only thing that made it possible at all was the fact that their life together was life in company with Christ. Until they had learned to be good together they would be good for very little, and until they had been taught together they would learn very little. Only an authentic community could possibly bear the appalling strain which destiny had in store for the Apostles.

Before Pentecost the principle that those who would live for Christ must hold together and keep themselves close was well established and understood, and after Pentecost the Church at once began to try to live and work in this way. At first, during the period covered by the book of the Acts in the New Testament, the apostles moved about in small groups. The different churches they founded in places like Antioch, Ephesus, and Corinth were all household churches. As long as Christianity was a proscribed religion there could be no church buildings, and congregations must always be small enough to be contained in a single room in a house. They were in fact sufficiently compact to become true communities, and to express all that is meant by the phrase, Togetherness in Christ. They were thus able to receive and to express so full a measure of the divine inspiration that the Church of the first three hundred years actually came near to being the living pattern of what the Old Testament writers had all the time seen with the eye of faith and hope, but had never actually experienced. History is the record of the power and the revolution-making love of these little companies of Christians. Within three hundred years, starting from scanty and unpromising beginnings, they had imposed their will upon the whole of the then known world. They did it because they so fully reflected and expressed the divine will, and they were able to achieve this tremendous feat largely because the shape of their organization set free the power of their personal Christian virtues.

Such, then, were the theological convictions from which we started. Any Christian who is convinced of the poverty of his own inspiration and the helpless weakness of his own power must meet these needs by yielding unconditionally to the Holy Spirit, and by doing this in company with other Christians who share his convictions. But this spiritual companionship must obviously be something deeper, more costly, more intimate, and more confidential than membership of a congregation can be expected to provide by itself. For a congregation is properly the whole body of the people of a parish at its worship, and it ought to include every kind of person, from babies in arms to great-grandmothers, in its ranks. Capacities so widely different can hardly be formed into the kind of community the Bible has in mind, and it is in practice perfectly possible, and indeed sadly usual, to be a regular and sincere member of the worshipping congregation and yet never to form any costly relationships within it. Relationships within the congregation can be, and commonly are, purely social; and many a devout communicant never speaks to any other communicant of spiritual things, but tries to live the Christian life alone and to face his spiritual problems in unaided solitariness. Of course it cannot be satisfactorily done, for from first to last the practice of Christianity is a corporate affair. It seemed, therefore, to follow that a congregation must give birth to smaller groups within itself if the inspiration of God was to descend upon it. In actual fact much of the work of the Church has always been done in this way.

From that point we started. Naturally we had the world's need and the Church's plain inability to meet that need constantly in our minds all the time. In 1942 how could it be otherwise? But the theological convictions did come first, and what we were really trying to do was to find the appropriate body to express them and bring them into fruitful relationship with each other in a twentieth-century setting.

Chapter Three

CONCEPTION AND BIRTH

No one could assent to this theological background without realizing that if any movement to express it had to be launched it must of necessity be the work of a group of people praying and acting together, and not of any individual. Right action must be the fruit of corporate and not of private judgment. It is true that a great deal, and perhaps most of the work of which some account is to be given in this chapter and the next was done by the author of this book, but this was because he was commissioned to do it by the group of clergy who were corporately the founders of S.C.K., and every step he took he referred to them before he took it. The origins of the whole thing were really different judgments, experiences, and impressions, some in one of our minds and some in another's. When they were put together they seemed to make a signpost pointing clearly to the way we thought we were called to go. But until the people had been brought together the ideas could not coalesce. The strange thing was that in 1941 when we were all thinking separately along much the same lines, most of us had never met one another, and at that time out of the group of six I myself knew only three. So everything had to wait until some chance event occurred which should not only collect us under the same roof but make it natural and

inevitable for us to find ourselves talking about these
things.

This chance event occurred in January 1942. It was
a four-day conference of clergy gathered from all over
the country which took place at a midland public school.
The subject of this conference does not concern us here
(actually it was to do with proposals for a large measure
of equalization of clerical incomes), for the chief thing
that came out of it had nothing to do with the purpose
for which it had been called. Most people at that conference must have carried away as their chief impression a memory of considerable discomfort. This was no
one's fault—certainly not the school's—and could not
possibly have been helped. But the snow lay deep on
the ground, and the central heating system suddenly
failed. Outside, the black-out made movement difficult
and even dangerous, and during the daytime the roads
of the town seemed all to be in use as a testing-ground
for new tanks, so that no one who addressed the conference had much chance of being heard by it. We had
to sleep in vast dormitories, in the roofs of which the
snow had found and exploited all the weak points. All
this is recalled only because it had a bearing on what
follows, and in a sense was its condition, and not in any
spirit of criticism of the school or the conference
authorities. They did all they could, but January 1942
was not a good time for conferences.

So it came about that one night found four of us
sitting late by a fire, and none of us very willing to go
to bed. We discussed the conference and were sure
that while what it hoped to do would go some way
towards meeting the most urgent evangelistic need of

the time, it could not possibly be expected to go very far. We needed some instrument more radical and much more spiritually basic than anything we could see coming out of that conference. Indeed we could not see anywhere existing at that moment quite the instrument or movement which the Church supremely needed if it was to bring the Gospel to all the people. The resources of the parochial system were quite manifestly insufficient, and must somehow be supplemented. But how? It was at this point that one of us turned the conversation so as to start at the other end. He began to enumerate biblical principles of inspiration instead of looking at the existing situation and assessing its needs, and much of what he said has already been written in the previous chapter. Another of us was impressed by the Cell Movement, then in its infancy, though he believed that if these cells were to be really effective they must be obedient to some discipline, and that they must somehow be joined together so as to make some pastoral oversight possible. A third was deeply under the influence of Mr. T. S. Eliot's book, *The Idea of a Christian Society*, with its prophetic underlining of our need to think as much of the society in which a man lives and of the general culture of which he is a part as of his own personal and individual soul. The fourth had had much experience of the power of small groups, and had himself been one of the pioneers of the way of reaching decisions by the use of a corporate waiting upon God. What we wanted, we all agreed, must contain all these features. The instrument to which the Bible seemed to point and which the needs of the day required was a series of small groups or cells of dedicated and disciplined Christian laymen, who would think and work out their discipleship in a thoroughly corporate way, and would by waiting upon God become exceedingly close-knit communities in Christ.

Time sped fast on that dark and cold night as we talked by the fire. Eventually there came a moment of silence. It was the silence which accentuates the wild surmise. Our discussion had been animated but academic. This was what we thought should be done, but presumably by somebody else. But what if it were we ourselves who were all the time being called to the laborious enterprise of manufacturing our own remedies? And what would it mean for us all if we were? At last one of us said in an almost casual voice, "Well, I suppose that means that we've got to do something about it." The curt phrase clinched it. We did not doubt that we had been "taken with a summons." After that it did not take long to decide what the first steps must be. We must somehow submit our judgment to the judgment of the Church, and if that wider and wiser judgment endorsed our own, there our unmistakable marching orders would be. But of course we could not approach the whole Church of England. We had no means of doing so. We could not even consult the present conference, for this was its last night. What we could do was to write a paper setting out our views, and then submit it to as wide and representative a body of churchpeople as possible, binding ourselves to accept the verdict of that body, whether it should be Refrain, or Wait, or Go Ahead. To-morrow we ourselves would be dispersed to our different posts, to Winchester, to Bristol, and to Peterborough. Our last decision, there-

fore was to charge one of our number to prepare and
submit the paper, and, if the verdict were what we
hoped it would be, to take on his shoulders the work
of carrying through the preparatory stages of the enterprise. It was the present author who was so charged.
He went apprehensively to bed and did not sleep very
much.

From the first, then, the whole enterprise was corporately conceived, and it was now to be corporately
executed. Though it was on my shoulders that the
bulk of the work fell (the pseudonyms of a studied im-
personality—"the present author"—become pretentious
at this point and must be abandoned) this was because
the weight was placed there by others. At no time from
then till now could what follows be credited to me or
any other single person. Both as dream and as fact
S.C.K. was ours. It was never mine, and it is not now,
nor ever will be.

I first enlarged the initiating company by bringing
into it a town and country priest from the diocese of
Winchester, and with their critical promptings at my
elbow I wrote a document which fully set out our views.
Reading it to-day I am rather horrified by its length.
It ran to eight quarto pages of duplicated single-space
typing, and it had a very eighteenth-century three-line
title, "A Design for an Active Order of Anglican Laity
for the Purpose of Providing the Church of England
with an Organized and Disciplined Body of Witnesses."
It went into action with a preliminary reference to Mr.
T. S. Eliot's *The Idea of a Christian Society*:

The book summed up a decade of Christian prophetic

thinking, the chief purpose of which has been to persuade us that if we must not think less about the Christian individual than we did, we must think far more about the society in which he lives and the general culture of which he is a part.

Then it summarized the conclusions of the prophetic analysts and went on:

But the time has come when this work of analysis and prophecy ought to pass over into whatever kind of remedial action it is which its findings imply. Already the prophets are fast becoming so discouraging as to stifle action: and already their stream of literature has reached the point where it is simply saying the same things over and over again. To make it creative we now need action.

But what kind of action? Something which strengthened and liberated the lay members of the Church to become the "new evangelistic army" in the places where they worked, and where the parochial clergy could hardly penetrate.

Evidently something more is needed. There is plainly a missing number, an X to be found and added to the existing equation of the Church. All this has naturally occurred to many other people, and quite a number of them have tried to "do something about it." Inevitably every group of reformers decides that X is something slightly different from what the group before it decided. Thus we have a multitude of experimental movements going on in the Church, most of which have begun since the outbreak of war. . . .

And then, to make an end of quoting from that immense letter, came the heart of the matter:

> When we take what the mathematicians call the Highest Common Factor of all these movements we find that they really consist of two pieces of insight—first, that religion to-day needs to come into the world out of a background of Christian Community, and second that the key to unlock the doors of indifference to religion is not so much in the possession of the clergy as of the laity. The lessons of the experiments at present being made, and any realistic reading of the facts of the religious situation in England, all point to one identical conclusion, that the Church needs a new kind of religious Order, the chief purpose of which is to provide, to guide, and to sustain the evangelistic witness of ordinary people leading ordinary lives.

The document continued for another six pages, but they contain nothing which is now of much importance, and most of the practical proposals about the conditions of membership of this Order which they suggested were altered out of all recognition as time went on.

It was certainly a portentous document, and well might the accompanying letter begin, "Although the amount of documents one gets sent in these days, with requests to read them, is something of a burden, I do none the less venture to ask you to read this." It speaks well for the patience and charity of Christian people that virtually everybody who received it did in fact read it, and that most of them wrote quite long letters about it. It went out on May 26th, 1942, to 160 people. I could not get enough paper to have any more copies made. The recipients were of all kinds, as complete a

cross-section of the Church as I could contain within
those limits. Several were journalists, and many were
teachers. There were novelists and sixth-form girls at
school. Some were soldiers and others were monks.
Many were bishops and clergy of many different types
and grades. I even had the hardihood to ask Dr.
Temple, the Archbishop of Canterbury, to read it, and,
as the event showed, he did. It was entirely characteristic of him that he wrote several letters about it, asked
me to come and see him and talk about it, and from
behind the scenes smoothed our path in many ways.
All these people were asked to say " with absolute frank-
ness" what they thought; and by their opinion we
undertook to abide. If most of them said, "This is no
good. Drop it," then drop it we would. But if they
said, "You've got something here. Go on with it,"
again we would be obedient. In the event, something
like ninety per cent said, "While this, that, and the
other detail is all wrong, nevertheless this is urgent,
basic, and right as a whole. For God's sake, go ahead."
No doubt was left. We had asked for our marching
orders and we had got them.

It would be a rather pointless interruption of the
narrative to include an abstract or anthology of the
various criticisms which the readers of this document
offered. There is a large and fat file of their letters. But
one criticism was almost universal, and must be men-
tioned here, for it proved to be prophetic, and from that
day to this it has been the greatest difficulty of all. I
had said that the Order could not be divorced from
the parochial system which is the normal unit of the
Church's organization. This, said one journalist, "is

a dismal prospect." The clergy themselves usually pre-
ferred the adjective Difficult. Indeed the difficulty was
felt by all the 160 people. It was essential, I had written,
to provide every company with a priest to advise, train,
and help them. Should he of necessity be the parish
priest? I had said Yes. My correspondents, clerical
as well as lay, with virtual unanimity said No. So the
suggestion was made that the priest-adviser should be
appointed by the Ruri-decanal Chapter, and that the
chosen man should look after every group in the
deanery. "I think this idea is good," wrote the Archbishop of Canterbury, partly because there will often be
individuals wishing to join from parishes where there
are not enough of them to make a unit, and it would
give them a choice of chaplain. If it were worked
through the Chapter, I do not think that any clergy
ought to have the smallest ground of complaint." Yes,
it was a good idea, but it did not happen. At the time
I seem to have taken refuge behind the common phrase,
"But we can tackle this later." In a way, we are tackling
it still!

All this activity of the pen went on steadily for the
first nine months of 1942, and after a time it really
became rather a daunting burden. But to it there had
to be added a great deal of railway travelling which, in
war time, was just as much a test of endurance to a
railway lover as to anyone else. Yet it was essential.
No movement is ever launched by sitting at a table
composing documents and writing letters. There must
also be endless consultations with all kinds of people.
They had to be as various in age and occupation as was
possible. Only by endless talks with as comprehensive

a cross-section of the whole Church of England as one man could manage personally to approach would it be possible to gauge something of how the Church as a whole would be likely to receive our proposals. So in these months I prowled round the country to places as various as Carlisle, Manchester, Burnley, Lincoln, Peterborough, Bristol, Cambridge, Rugby, and (over and over again) London. At the end of it all, in October 1942, we all thought the time had come to put all this preliminary work to the test of submission to a conference, and this invitation was sent out:

While there is plainly the need of a great deal more prayer and consultation, we must not let that necessary stage go on indefinitely, but should set a time limit to it. I therefore propose for your acceptance that we, that is, those who receive this letter, should come together for a four-day conference in January 1943. I don't yet know where this conference can be, but no doubt I can find somewhere. It would be the business of this conference to do three main things:

1. To go very carefully into all the criticisms made.
2. To produce at least the outlines of a workable constitution.
3. To decide what should be done next.

I do hope you will do all you can to arrange to come. In the meantime we should be gathering, each one of us, all the opinion we can get so that when we meet we can really feel that we have done what we can to take the measure of Church opinion as a whole.

The invitation went to about fifty people. About half

c

of them were clergy, and these included all the members
of the original group. The rest went to such lay people
as had shown special interest, and a very mixed collection they were. Most of them were young men and
women, several of them in the Services. There were
engineers and journalists, authors and playwrights,
teachers and musicians, nurses, dons, and housewives.
Hardly any of them were the sort of people normally
found at pious gatherings out of church. Only a very
few had ever been to a conference of any sort in all
their lives, and in the event their inexperience of the
way any conference works proved to be an embarrassment as well as a gain, but the gain predominated. At
any rate, when we saw them all assembled at St. Hugh's
College, Oxford, on that first night, we knew that it was
from the likes of them that any Order which could hope
to fulfil our vision must be formed, and we were content to rest it all on their free decisions, first to choose
the form of it themselves, and then to decide whether
the time was ripe to go forward. Their inexperience
of this kind of work was, however, very obvious, and
we were thankful that we had the Bishop of Hereford
(Dr. R. G. Parsons) as chairman. It was in any case
necessary to have a bishop with us, to represent the
episcopal bench. As time wore on we were no less
thankful for the skill, devotion, and charm of the girl
who had undertaken to be the secretary of the conference, and was later to become the first secretary of
S.C.K. She was and she continued to be a real find,
and this has been just as true of every secretary who
has succeeded her.

A document setting out the conclusions at which we

had arrived and suggesting the kind of problem to which the conference would have to address itself was sent out to its members in advance. But in the event nobody took much notice of it. This first S.C.K. Conference was prophetically characteristic of all that have followed it. Those who plan it say what it should try to do and then it goes and does something entirely different. So it was in January 1943. It split itself into small groups and tried to write a constitution and reached chaos. It met as a single body and tried to write a Rule of Life and to find a title, and reached chaos. They all meant so well and were so kind, and the very benevolence and good intention did but tie the very tangles into knots. Before we ever began we bound ourselves to accept nothing and to do nothing unless we could carry the whole body with us; only unanimity and nothing less than unanimity could authorize decision and initiate action. After two days of it, it looked as if nothing could save our dreams, as if the whole vision must peter out in confusion before it had ever been born. In our despair, some of us were beginning to think seriously of calling the whole thing off, packing our bags and going home. The marvel and the hope was that nobody ever got cross or spoke rudely.

Truly we all had a lot to learn, and there was nobody to teach us. But the first lesson of all was that if you call the sort of conference which confers and doesn't listen to speeches, if it consists of people who are nearly all unused to conferences and few of whom have ever met each other before, if you set it to tackle an inevitably difficult piece of pioneering work in which there are no precedents to rely on, and if you then say that

nothing less than absolute and freely arrived at
unanimity will count, then chaos is what you will infallibly get—unless the programme allows for quite long
daily periods of silent prayer all together. But if there
is a sufficiency of silent corporate prayer, then you will
almost never fail to arrive at unanimity in the end, so
long as everyone keeps their head and their temper.
Our mistake was that we had provided for no silent
prayer at all; and though in the years to come we have
made innumerable mistakes, at least we have never
again made that one.

On the second evening the chaos was as impenetrable
as ever, and everybody was so tired that the conversation flagged slowly, died, and there was a great hush.
Then it was that one of the women began slowly to
speak. "It's no use our going on like this," she said,
"we shall never get anywhere. The trouble about this
conference is that it is strong on resolve but weak on
prayer. As a body we've never prayed this thing out
together. We've been so busy making our human plans
that we've never tried to listen to the Holy Spirit. So
I suggest, first, that we now say Compline and go to
bed. I suggest, second, that we resolve to scrap completely all we've done so far. It just isn't good enough
for anything worth having to come of it. Then I suggest that to-morrow morning we keep silence in chapel,
and simply say our prayers about it all until lunch,
and after that start all over again." Perhaps it might
be counted for righteousness that although half the time
of the conference had gone, the course she suggested
was immediately agreed upon by everybody. The
whole of the next morning, from 10 to 12.30, we spent

in silence and in prayer. It was an effort especially for those, the majority, who had never been asked to do anything like this before, but it eased the general strain. The confused heats of our desire faded and were turned into the coolness of a deeper peace.

After that we never looked back. We sent the laity into a room by themselves, with no parson present, and bade them decide whether the Order was to be confined to Anglicans or to be for all Christians of all Churches. So determined were they not to produce something vague and well-meaning but colourless, and so sure that whatever we built must stand solidly on sacramental foundations, that they decided that none but Anglican communicants could be members. We asked them next to produce the shortest possible draft of a workable constitution for an Order consisting of ordinary people leading ordinary workaday lives but organized with the group and not the individual as the unit. It was astonishing how quickly they did it. But they had the wisdom to make the authors and journalists among them do the actual drafting. At the same time the clergy went off by themselves. One group of them quite quickly reduced sixteen previous drafts of the Rule to an agreed short and simple statement, while another applied itself to what the functions and powers of the priest-adviser of each group should be, and how he should be appointed. In all this what had before proved impossible now seemed quite easy.

Next morning—the last morning—all this work done separately by the laity and clergy was submitted to the whole conference and with very little discussion was unanimously approved. The choice of a title was troublesome, for every suggestion made that was not frivolous proved to be a title which some other society already possessed. At last a previously silent member in a corner said in a sepulchral voice, "Why not The Servants of Christ the King? Servants—because that is all we are or ever hope to be: Christ the King—because that is what He both is and must become if there's to be any hope for the world, and because He came to found a Kingdom: He said so again and again. Besides, S.C.K. are nice, easy initials to remember."

So at last the vision took its shape. It was to be an Order of a new kind, an Order for ordinary lay people, communal and disciplined like all its very different historic forbears, but not uniformed, with promises of obedience but not of celibacy or poverty. It had its rule by which every member was solemnly bound for twelve months, and renewable at will every year thereafter. The Rule read, and still reads:

Believing that my life in all its fullness—possessions, personal relationships, time and actions—belongs to God, I hereby reaffirm the promises made for me at Holy Baptism and renewed by me at Confirmation. I believe that God has called me as a Servant of Christ the King through prayer, discipline and fellowship to spread His Kingdom. I therefore hold myself bound by the following obligations, and by the Rule of my Company:

1. To worship at least once a week in Church, however difficult that may be, to receive Holy Communion regularly and frequently, to spend a definite time daily in prayer and Bible reading, and to learn ever more of the Christian Faith.

2. To seek through the Company, to which I belong, and through every means in my power, to draw others into the fellowship of the Church, and to claim for the Rule of Christ every part of human life, both in my country, and throughout the world.

3. To be a loyal member of the Anglican Communion in the province and diocese in which I live, and to be obedient to the unanimous decisions of my Company.

It had its outward shape—companies of not less than three or more than twelve, each one with a priest to be its adviser, and with his powers and limitations of power carefully defined. It had its inward spirit, the obligations of unanimity and of Waiting upon God as the essential prelude of all action. It had the bare bones of a system of administration whereby all the companies which might form could be held together and in touch with each other in a single fellowship. It was carefully tied into the organized life of the Church since the Archbishops were to be asked to recognize it by appointing the Warden and one of the bishops to be the Visitor, and by the requirement that every company must be accepted by the diocesan bishop before it could be recognized as an S.C.K. company.

Only one more question remained. Would the conference agree that we might now start to use this instrument even though it was obvious that we really knew remarkably little about it? Or ought we to wait for another twelve months and use that period to choose and train a sufficient number of priests to be the advisers of the companies? For a long time the debate ranged round these alternatives, and opinion seemed

evenly divided. We had a very anxious hour. But in
the end the younger lay people present held with such
passion the conviction that it was now or never, and
that they were in positions where they desperately
needed precisely this kind of help, that the more
cautious, emphasizing once more the risks we were
taking, agreed that it was right we should take them.
And after all we could learn only by trying: there was
no other way. So the Warden, the present writer, was
appointed, or, rather, commended, to the Archbishops
for their approval.

Thus the Servants of Christ the King had at last been
brought to birth in one of the most agonizing and yet
fortifying experiences many of us had ever known. Yet
the fact that in all those most tiring and exacting
four days, and through all the disappointments and
anxieties, the whole conference never once fell below
the high level of genuinely Christian community,
never once failed in charity, courtesy, or patience, and
that each member co-operated to the fullness of his
ability with all the rest, was perhaps an augury which
gave us confidence as well as a measure of humility.
It was all too true and too obvious that we had much
to learn about conferences, and all to learn about the
work which this conference had initiated. But at least
it had not wholly lacked the quality which the New
Testament calls Grace.

Chapter Four

THE FIRST EXPERIMENTAL YEAR

So there we were. We had been given a vision of what
might be done for the Kingdom of God in England if
in every place where men lived and worked there was
a small group of dedicated and disciplined Christians
embedded among them, and if such a group lived its
life as closely to New Testament standards as the conditions of twentieth-century England at war allowed.
We had, as we were bound to believe, been called by
God to try to create such groups, but this summons was
conditional upon our submission to the inspiration of
the Holy Spirit every inch of the way, and to this condition we had tried to give obedience. All this had borne
its tentative fruit—tentative because though the Order
was in existence it still had no members, but only a
warden and a secretary, and two groups of people, one
at Brierfield, in Lancashire, and the other at Girton
College, in Cambridge, which had already begun on an
unofficial and experimental basis. We had very nearly
forgotten that we had no money either, but at the last
session of the conference somebody suddenly remem-
bered the fact, so we passed round the hat then and
there, and when the money was counted we could hardly
believe our eyes, for it amounted to no less than £66.
That money was certainly a sacrament of goodwill and
faith, and these were after all the indispensable condi-

tions of our being able to do anything worth while, and we have them behind us still.

The Warden was given his orders to go ahead from that point. But this was the only positive order he had. The rest of his instructions were all prohibitions, but they were emphatic. He must not make any attempt to justify his position by strenuously struggling to produce the results which would look well in a printed report of his work. If he was judged at all it would be on the quality of the companies, not on their quantity. Therefore he must not make desperate efforts to "get S.C.K. going." The companies must form naturally; they must not be hustled and overpersuaded into existence. By the same token there must be no publicity; no articles must be written and no broadcasts must be made to call any attention to S.C.K. The Order was to be the hidden handmaid of the Church. If people asked to be told about it, naturally one would go to tell them, but they must not be asked to join; the asking must be done by them. Furthermore, the Warden was not to be a money-raiser, and no company was ever to be asked for any definite subscription. Nor have they been, but in ten years we have always had just enough for what we needed, and never very much over.

The Archbishops gave us their welcome and their blessing in warm terms, and they appointed the Bishop of Ely (Dr. Edward Wynn) to be the Visitor, which office he still holds. Thus S.C.K. became a recognized if still a hidden part of the life of the Church and was suffi-ciently dovetailed into its normal organization. All our early efforts to extend our sketchy skeleton of an organization beyond this point came to naught. We began by asking the bishops to appoint a warden in each diocese, and though with one exception they were willing enough to do this and took real pains over it, yet the system of diocesan wardens only worked when the warden in question had been in at the birth of S.C.K. by being present at its initiating conference. It was just as well that this early effort to produce an organization failed, but the failure pointed to one of the chronic difficulties which have beset our path from the beginning. It is the difficulty, almost the impossibility, of making a cold-blooded explanation convey the real point to the listener. You can convey the need, but you cannot explain the method of waiting upon God as adequately meeting the need. To the natural question, what would these companies actually do? you can answer only, whatever the Holy Spirit tells them to do. It is admittedly a dusty answer, and yet it is the whole point. To the question, what exactly is this S.C.K.— a society, a movement, a fellowship, a prayer group, a study group, a ginger group? You can only answer, All of them and also none of them. S.C.K. in fact is something which has to be experienced before it can be fully understood, and explanation cannot do much more than awake the desire to take a chance and try.

In spite of all its heats and perturbations the initiating conference had been just such an experience and therefore it was natural that every one of the first companies should owe its foundation to somebody who had been present at it. Very soon they began to come in. In the first year Bristol had six or seven, one of which consisted of diocesan lay officials. Swindon started with two companies, one of women working in factories and the railway service and the other consisting of clergy wives. Two companies were quickly started among girls in the A.T.S., and another on an R.A.F. station near Rugby. Winchester had two companies, and so did Ipswich. There were others at Kendal, Norwich, Lincoln, Cambridge, and one among undergraduates at King's College, London. To go round and visit them all was a moving experience. One had dreamed of this for years, and behold, there the dream was, shaped in flesh and blood before one's very eyes. Privilege indeed!

These early companies (we called them companies in order to avoid calling them cells or groups) were nearly all formed after this manner. A member of the conference would have some friends whom he would call together and to whom he would describe what we had done. Was this, he would ask them, the sort of thing they were looking for? Rarely, if ever, did they make their decision then and there, and they were in fact discouraged from doing so. But sometimes, after an interval for thought and prayer, two or three of them met again for more discussion. This would often reveal that they were sharing a concern or a perplexity about some person, or some cause, or for some particular development of parish evangelistic work. Then one of them might think of someone else, or two or three more, whom he knew to be concerned about the same thing. They quickly realized that they could serve it better if they served it together, especially if this togetherness was deeply grounded in a common obedience to each other and to the Holy Spirit as in an

S.C.K. company it was bound to be. After that the formation of the company was fairly easy, though there would generally be a period of cold feet in which their fear of launching was greater, or more immediate to their consciousness, than their desire, but in the end desire practically always conquered fear, and so they took the plunge and a new company was born.

Even in that first year there seemed no limit to the variety of these " concerns." A deep interest in missions in China brought together two of the earliest companies. Service companies were always welded together by two motives—the desire of their members to keep their own Christian obligations bright and shining in the very difficult conditions of Service life, and a certain dismay at the amount of indifference to Christianity in their own units. Perhaps most of them were concerned chiefly that the quality of the witness of their own parish churches was less high than they thought it might become. Others again set out to find the way to take the Gospel into the place where they worked and the community they found there. Very, very few of them knew more clearly than this why God had called them to this form of discipleship. They just believed that He had. They had their general concern, but no idea at all of what to do about it. But at this stage it was not their business to know. God would tell them when He saw they were ready to be used. In the meantime their business was to yield to be made a tiny but usable community and offer that to God for His pleasure. The rest would follow. In the event what these and all subsequent companies were led to do was almost never what they had supposed when they began. It was the-inevitable consequence of their having accepted a vocation to an undisclosed purpose.

The early history of one particular company may best illustrate the general outline of how companies form and start their corporate life, though this company was not one of the early ones. A rural parish of green fields and woods with a village church and a village outlook became almost overnight the scene of an enormous oil refinery. Houses were hurriedly built in the fields, and very soon many hundreds of workers and their families, brought from every corner of Britain, were living there and facing the adventure of starting life again in totally novel surroundings. They far outnumbered the original village people. The vicar duly visited them all, and the results of his visitation were less daunting then he expected, for though the great mass of these workers exhibited the usual indifference to religion, there were a number of the younger technicians and their wives who were regularly coming to his church. But there were not enough of them to count for much in the vital thing which had to be done, the welding of the new factory and its workers into the life of the Church in the village. It was at this point that the vicar heard of S.C.K., and thought it was the very thing that these young technicians needed. They consisted of one of the Works doctors, a research chemist, a transport manager, and two engineers, and between them they were familiar with every department of the factory and with every one of its workers. He called them together, and their wives with them, and told them about it. Not for several months did they make up their minds. Their hesitations were due to two causes—they feared that they "might not be able to live up to the standard," and they wished their wives to come in with them, which, as every one of them was the mother of a young baby, created the complication that there would have to be two separate rules of life.

Eventually they made their decision, and formed themselves into two companies, which would often but not always meet together, having the one concern of trying to represent the Church both in the factory and in the homes and families of its workers. Now what did this mean for them in actual practice? First of all, as one of them said, "We are all friends now, but we shall have to learn this friendship all over again at a much deeper level." To do this they must meet together regularly, and therefore must fix a regular rhythm of meetings which, once unanimously agreed, must be a matter of obligation. They must learn to be obedient to Christ in and through their obedience to each other, and so must construct a rule of life which all could keep. They must learn to pray together, and so must be a prayer group. They must know their Christian doctrine and how it fits on to life, and so must be a study group. They must get to know each other so well and to rely on each other so completely that in their talk they could move from frivolity to devoutness and back again without any sense of awkwardness or incongruity. They must bring and hold this together in regular periodic meetings for waiting upon God after the manner to be fully described in Chapter V of this book, and they must take no decision for action except by this way of waiting upon God. To help them to learn all this was the responsibility of their vicar who was their adviser. It would all take time, but they must be prepared to give that time, for with them as with all new companies, at least the first six months were to be regarded as a period of preparation and training. They had accepted a vocation of which only the strategic aim was clear while the tactical methods of pursuing it remained undisclosed. But all this time, and from the very moment of their first forming, they were a fully fledged S.C.K. company, with all the rights and duties of all other companies, and equal in status with the oldest on the list.

We came to the end of that first year with some thirty-five companies on the list, and we were under obligation to gather an S.C.K. conference again at Oxford at Epiphany 1944, where the lessons of the first experimental year might be assessed and the mistakes corrected. Fifty people, both clergy and laity, duly assembled, and they were an exceedingly mixed gathering, representing between them many different ways of life. This time we had our Visitor, the Bishop of Ely, with us.

Now S.C.K., considered as a single body, lives largely on its conferences. They are the only means we have of bringing the whole movement together in one place, and in them is vested the whole government of it. Any major change of policy must be proposed to and accepted by the conference before it can be put into effect. Exactly the same obligation which a company has of reaching decisions unanimously or not reaching them at all is laid on the conference. Unanimity has to be wrested out of the fifty to seventy people present, and every voice, every second thought, every last-minute doubt or hesitation, must be cheerfully heard and seriously considered. On paper it ought to lead to chaos, and at the first conference it very nearly did, but never once since then have we failed to reach unanimity on any problem which mattered. But if a conference of fifty or more people is to accept such a principle as binding, it must do its work and live its corporate life in a certain way. It must be a conference which confers, not one which listens to speeches by experts. It must spend—and this is the most vital point of all—a high proportion of its time on its knees in prayer and worship. It must not be worked too hard, and there must be plenty of free time every day. It must be warm, comfortable, and decently fed. Those who have to organize and plan it must not mind if the conference suddenly takes the bit between its teeth, throws their plans and agenda on to the dust heap, and rearranges its own procedure, for this constantly happens. Above all it must reach its decisions by waiting upon God for them.

At first most of our conferences took place round about Epiphany, and lasted three full days. But in more recent years we have found it better to accept the most gracious hospitality of St. Swithun's School, Winchester, for a full week in August. It is possible in this way to have far more members, and to give far more free time; and one is so much less driven and harried by the limitations of time. But the daily time-table of the conference is in principle much the same. The day begins with Holy Communion. After breakfast and before any work is done, the whole body gathers in chapel and spends half an hour in silent prayer and meditation. After that we work in small groups till

D

lunch time. In the summer everyone is then left completely free until supper, but in the winter work is resumed after tea. These periods of work in groups, by the way, are often punctuated by short intervals of silence. Then after supper the whole conference gathers together, and what is done then is not a continuance of the day's work so much as random reflections on its wider implications, to which the members contribute much as the spirit moves them. Then after a cup of tea the day ends with compline in the chapel and a short address by the bishop or chaplain. The last night of all is always spent in corporate "fun and games."

Such are the bare bones of our conferences. It is much harder to describe their spirit, yet this is what makes them so memorable. I have been to scores of conferences of one sort or another, yet never to any in which people of all kinds, many of them strangers to each other when they arrive, become so quickly and so completely members one of another. It always seems as though for that one week we were really living as Christians were always meant to live, with worship, prayer, work and play exactly balanced; and it all seems so natural and so easy and so right. It soon becomes quite difficult to remember that there is another world outside which rules its life by very different standards. Very occasionally someone may bring in a newspaper and others may glance at the headlines. They seem to be giving news of a world as remote as the planet Mars.

There is no doubt whatever about the joy. Sixty-five of us live, pray, work and play together for a full week. We are an exceedingly mixed collection, rich and poor, young and old, really and truly one with another. Inevitably, therefore, it is happy. Trying to do the will and to be the children of God together is always the happiest thing which can happen to anybody. The conference becomes for all of us a sheer happiness which will not easily fade. Perhaps the best testimonies to this are sentences from two private letters, each of which was written by someone who had never been to one of our conferences before. One of them wrote: "Perhaps the best way to say Thank you is by telling you that it was the loveliest and happiest week that I have ever spent, and that, of course, is the natural outcome of living in such a loving community." The other, who came straight from a host of trouble to Winchester, wrote: "To me it was a wonderful and amazing experience from the very beginning to find myself within a community in which it was possible to be completely natural with not just the few with whom one felt an exceptional kinship, but with each individual. In fact the impact of Christian fellowship was so great that instead of feeling weary and worn there was at once a sense of renewal and refreshment."

None of this, I think, is overstated, and it faithfully describes the atmosphere of all our conferences. Moreover, it will quite infallibly be the experience of every conference which mingles worship, work, play, and mutual charity of behaviour in their due proportion. The real secret is that you must never, never, no matter how strong the temptation, cut down the time given to prayer and worship, nor steal periods from the free time, because you are getting hard pressed to finish the work and the time is running short.

The 1944 conference endorsed what we had done in the first experimental year, after a full report had been made of it.   But it made four decisions, three positive and one negative, which between them completed the shape and outline of S.C.K.   In future we were to be allowed to have junior or preparatory companies of boys and girls between sixteen and eighteen years old, and also companies consisting of clergymen only.   The junior companies were not to be allowed to make any formal promises, and no one under eighteen could be a full member; and it still remained the rule that no clergyman could be a member of a lay company and " vice versa."   In practice there have been very few junior companies, never more than two at any one time. To-day there is only one, but this one consists of the members of a large boys' club and the whole club has been transformed by this group at its centre steadily practising this way of Christian discipleship.   Nor has there at any time been more than three or four companies of clergymen, but the day on which we extended a lay organization to include the clergy was indeed a fortunate one, as will be realized by those who read Chapter VIII of this book.   The third positive decision has also proved to be a condition of health.   It was that every single holder of office in S.C.K., from that of the Warden and Secretary downwards to every company leader, is bound to offer his resignation every twelve months and submit himself unconditionally to the free choice of his fellows between re-election and replacement.   In practice no re-election has ever been automatic, and many companies change their leaders every year as a matter of principle.

The fourth and negative decision was much more difficult, and though it was made unanimously, as it always must be, there are still many of us who are not wholly convinced that it was right. It was to drop the word Order from the title, and to cease to speak of ourselves as an Order. From the beginning we had all been clear that we must not use the phrase Religious Order, since lay people living non-celibate and gainfully employed lives in the ordinary world cannot be "Religious" in the technically ecclesiastical and monastic sense of that word. A monk or a nun is a Religious. Any other Christian is religious, or should be, but not A Religious. But while that was always clear, it had seemed to us that there was need of an altogether new kind of Order, quite different from the "Third Orders" of established Religious Orders, and this was what we had tried to build. Moreover the word Order has a bite, a drive, and an inexorable definiteness about it, which words like Society, Movement, and Fellowship have not. The word Society suggests something quite easy to belong to, while the word Order suggests something much harder, and intrinsically more worth while. All this was quite clear to us, and yet it was undeniable that our use of the word Order had in fact created an uncommon amount of misunderstanding of our function and purpose. A number of instances were given where real damage had been done by it. But what really clinched the matter was the difficulty, even the impossibility of defining where the difference lay between the obligations proper to a Society and those proper to the kind of Order that we had in mind. We could not see that there was any difference. We tried very hard and persistently to find sentences to take the threefold monastic vow of Celibacy, Poverty, and Obedience and redraft them so as to be practicable for the highly diverse kinds of people of whom our companies consisted. It proved to be quite impossible, except in the case of Obedience where the third clause in the General Rule of S.C.K. offered a perfectly satisfactory adaptation and paraphrase. So it seemed that to persist in the use of the word Order was being unrealistic and even defiantly idealistic, and we sadly and reluctantly dropped it. Were we right? I wish I was perfectly sure.

Thus we ceased to be an Order. But we never found another word to use instead. What *is* S.C.K.—a society, a movement, a fellowship? To this day we have never been able to win unanimous agreement to any of these words.

Chapter Five

WAITING UPON GOD

An earlier chapter outlined the theology on which this whole venture of discipleship was based, and claimed that through all the ten years we had been consistently faithful to it. But what has kept us faithful was the enshrining of this theology in a particular method of expressing corporate loyalty to it called Waiting upon God, and the insistence of one conference after another that every single company claiming to belong to S.C.K. must accept the obligation of its periodical but regular use. We had to make ourselves be firm and faithful in renewing this demand, for no company has ever found waiting upon God easy. It is one of those things which look simple enough on paper but which need a great deal of learning. Yet no one has ever suggested that it should cease to be imposed on all the companies. Though many of us have found it a strange and bewildering exercise, we all continue to hold ourselves to it and to try.

We should not have done this merely because it was good discipline, nor yet because when the companies are geographically widely scattered and exceedingly varied in the kinds of people they contain it is obviously useful to have some one formal act which all alike must perform. These are both real needs, but no doubt we could have devised something less exacting to meet them. We held ourselves to it for deeper reasons than these. The first is that waiting upon God does more than anything else whatsoever to take a number of individuals and make them into a close-knit fellowship, and this by enhancing rather than denying the individuality of each one of them. The second is that no other ritual so completely brings into focus the particular insights for which S.C.K. stands, the initiative of God through the Holy Spirit, our dependence on Him, the right and free use of our reason, and our togetherness in Christ in absolute equality with one another. If an S.C.K. company is " different " it is waiting upon God that makes it so, for it is through this that it receives its individuality, its colour, its real life, and its soul.

Waiting upon God is in essence a corporate rhythm of devotion which has three stages. First there is the period of silent prayer and meditation, in which no word is spoken, and which lasts for a given, predetermined time. In this period the company places itself and all its members at the disposal of the Holy Spirit. But almost always it does this in the context, so to say, of its own common concern. It brings before God some part or stage of the unfolding or development of this concern, and in seeking to learn the will of the Holy Spirit about it it places the minds and wills of its members at His disposal. It empties itself to be filled by Him in and through the concern it places before Him. This is followed by a controlled discussion in which each person in turn says whatever he may have been given to say, or whatever may be in his mind, and no one may interrupt him or speak out of his turn.

Thus you get every contribution out on the table in full view. The third stage of the rhythm sifts and sorts these contributions by free and uncontrolled discussion. It is at this point that the office of the leader becomes all important. He must gently steer the discussion towards the area of agreement, and do it without even seeming to dominate it. This discussion continues until a common mind or judgment emerges, which very often may be no more than a common perplexity. If it is, then they repeat the process with this perplexity as the theme until, sooner or later, the perplexity itself becomes a unanimous conviction. When at last it does, the conviction or decision is written down and offered to God, and they can reasonably say that they believe this or propose to do this " because it seems good to the Holy Ghost and to us."

Now this must surely be the right way for Christians to search corporately for their convictions and decisions, because it is so profoundly and ineradicably scriptural. In the Bible waiting upon God appears in at least four different senses:

1. As in Psalm 62 and Psalm 123, verse 2, where the sense is that of waiting in stillness for divine deliverance from trouble, so that here waiting upon God is the condition of hope.
2. Waiting for instructions or guidance or what to do, as St. Paul waited after his conversion in the vision on the Damascus road.
3. Waiting to receive the enlightenment, or a renewal of vitality, as the disciples so often sat at the feet of Jesus; and here the sense is not that of waiting for the solution of a problem.

4. Waiting for an expected and particular event to take place, as the Apostles did before Pentecost, or the Ten Virgins in the Parable.

Waiting upon God is therefore impoverished if used only in the second of these senses, though no doubt it is bound to be used in this sense more often than in any of the other three. But fundamentally the reason why a company waits together upon God is to receive its life from Him, and to offer its life to Him. It follows that its members should come to it not too conscious of their own ideas, but should be "heavy with desire" to offer to God one more instrument for Him to use in the world in His own way and in His own time. So used, there is no single thing we do which waiting upon God does not enrich. But what experience shows to be particularly enriched by it is our sense of the Holy Spirit, who in this way, as hardly in any other, becomes a real person to us, with a personality and character of His own. He steps out of the realm of being a vague and shadowy influence, and becomes as vividly real to us as is our Lord Himself.

Although this method of waiting upon God is more difficult than a bare description of it sounds, its merits are very obvious. Without something like it, it is hard indeed to see how the vital principles of dependence upon the initiative of God through the Holy Spirit, and a right, free and equal use of our reason, could possibly be combined. Whether its purpose is to arrive at a decision about a problem, or simply to yield to be filled with whatever form of life or vitality the Holy

Spirit chooses to give, or to bring the corporate study of the Scriptures under light of His teaching about them, the fact remains that it is always begun with a period of corporate and silent prayer and meditation. This can hardly fail to suggest to all who take part in it certain vital truths about the perpetual relationship of God and Man. The word "guidance" may be somewhat compromised in these days, but that fact should not conceal from us the truth that God does want to guide us. He can only do so if we ask Him for it and wait in silence to receive it. It is this which more than anything else distinguishes an S.C.K. company from a committee. The concern of the committe is chiefly with the form of its activity, but the first concern of any group which arrives at its decisions by Waiting upon God is to receive its life from Him. The form of activity which this may lead to is of secondary importance to that.

But the Holy Spirit does want to guide us into right action for Him. He must obviously know the answer to all the problems which baffle and beset us, and must yearn to tell that answer to us. But we are bound to pass any inspiration we think we receive from Him through the sieve of our human reason. History is littered with the disasters which happen when sincere Christians are mistaken about the guidance of God, and since we must always receive His light through glasses which are cracked and distorted by sin, mistakes are almost inevitable. But we may have confidence that if a corporate body uses to the full its members' reason upon any such promptings; if it accepts nothing which it cannot accept unanimously;

and if on top of that it has to submit its decisions to the independent judgment of the priest who is its adviser, then what still survives these three filters is at least very likely to be the authentic bidding or teaching of the Holy Spirit!   Then again, there is no other method than the controlled discussion by which the absolute equality of all the members can be asserted and protected.   The over-talkative and the specially dynamic cannot possibly dominate the proceedings and the naturally dumb get an equal chance with them.   As a matter of fact, consistently observed over ten years, there is nothing which is so powerful to create true fellowship in Christ.

So it is that the S.C.K. company arrives at its decisions and so it is that it reconciles any differences or strain between its members.   In this setting, and in this setting alone, it is really possible to speak the truth in love and to increase the amount of love available by doing so.   There may be a danger of taking a mechanical view of guidance, though in practice this danger is so fully recognized and guarded against that it almost never happens.   There may be, and there certainly is, much to be learned at every point, and especially in the right use of the opening period of silence.   There is a still further difficulty in that this method was really worked out by a group of priests some years before S.C.K. was born, with the idea that those practising it would have a full thirty-six hours for the purpose, whereas the enormous majority of our companies have to telescope the whole rhythm into perhaps a couple of hours in the evening.   So it is that over and over again, in one conference after another, we have had to spend a great deal of the time in giving instruction about it and in the actual practice of it. Yet throughout we have held ourselves firmly to this blessed discipline, and as long as S.C.K. remains in existence at all, so long shall we continue with it.

Chapter Six

WHAT THE COMPANIES DO

ALMOST from the beginning it has been our custom at S.C.K. conferences to open them by asking the representative of each company present to give a five-minute account of the life and work of his company. One after another they stand up and begin rather apologetically by saying that they really have nothing very exciting to report, except that . . . and then there follows a rather deprecating reference to things like the remodelling of a Sunday School, the preparation and after-care of confirmation candidates, the organizing of and the visiting for a mission, or some adventure of standing firmly for righteousness. After that, and without exception, they say that the Christian fellowship they have found has been of a depth and quality they had never found before, and that it has become so precious and strengthening to them that they would now be dismayed if they had to do without it.

Such is the little speech made twenty times or more by one person after another, and at first it all seems a little tame and pedestrian. But then, little by little, a pattern or a composite picture emerges from all these mosaics of ordinary Christian service, and one sees that when added together they really amount to something rather big. That stand for righteousness in a factory given over to dirty language and the corruption of young boys was not really a little unimportant thing; and that youthful company in a suburban parish, which during a very prolonged vacancy in the vicarage took over the whole of the preparation of two sets of confirmation candidates was doing something quite big with destiny.   At any rate the recitation leaves no doubt at all that if none of these various pieces of work had been done, the Church that year must have been far less effective than it was, and the Kingdom of God by that much impoverished; and all of them were such that only a group of dedicated people could have done them.

It is very probable that small faithfulnesses count for more in the economics of the Kingdom of God than mighty works.   There are, after all, so many more of them.   But the mighty, or at any rate the exciting, works are there too.   In those first six or seven years many exciting and in their results astonishing adventures were undertaken in obedience to the promptings of the Holy Spirit, and by the most apparently unlikely companies.   What ought to have happened, one would think, was that the adventures would come the way of the companies consisting of the young and ardent, while the more middle-aged ones would get the duller and more pedestrian jobs.   In actual practice it was often exactly the other way round.   Most of the ventures which caught the eye, the forlorn hopes which formed the only possible news stories which a journalist would look at, fell to the lot of the companies which contained the more experienced Christians.   The five which follow are only a sample of others which might equally well have been told had this book been longer than it is intended to be.

There was, in a large industrial city, a company of teachers—it still exists. There were six of them, and all of them were completely dependent on what they earned. From the first they had no doubt that whatever their work would eventually turn out to be, it was bound to be something to do with religious education. But month after month went by without their being able to see quite where their company was intended to fit into it, or what tiny corner of it was, in the providence of the Holy Spirit, reserved for them. Eventually they arrived at what looked like a position of complete stalemate. "It's no good going on talking and talking about religious education. We've done that for nearly a year. It's time we did something." But what? Then came the inspiration. They knew that one of their members had for years dreamed of going to St. Christopher's College to be trained so that she might give her life to this work. But it had never been financially possible. They were inspired to ask her whether she would allow the Company to make itself responsible for sending her there, and seeing her through. If she would accept this, it should be their task as an S.C.K. company. They broke up in something of a "wild surmise," the one member to pray it out, the others to make enquiries and do sums. Eventually they discovered that it would cost about £300 in all. It was a formidable shock, but they were not daunted. One member said she would advance the sum from her savings: she knew it would come back. The others bound themselves to be responsible for it.

The girl, after several days of prayer and thought, came
to the knowledge that she must accept, and did so.
Her heroism was not less than theirs, and in taking
she also gave. It was this apparently impossible venture
which finally put that company on its feet and established it firmly. They called to their aid the other
companies in the district, and in an astonishingly short
space of time they raised the whole of that £300, some of
which went to compensate the parents for the wages
the girl would have to forgo during her training. She
went to St. Christopher's and is now doing the work of
a diocesan Sunday School Organizer on which her heart
had been set. She herself could hardly believe it. "I
am doing work I have longed to do for a very long
time," she wrote, "among those I know and love, and
I cannot believe that it is really me doing it." There
is a colophon to that story. After the girl had passed
through her training and was established in her job,
the same company, its appetite whetted, decided that
it must now raise enough money to see a young
working man through the whole of his training as
a candidate for Holy Orders. This, too, they did,
and the young man is now at work in an industrial
parish.

Another company found itself suddenly pitchforked
into a very different kind of venture, the pattern of
which—one member actually doing the work while the
others stay at home and say the prayers—constantly
recurs. This company consists of women working in
various factories in the town, and most of them were
members of their Trades Union. One of the members
attended a Trades Union meeting which was addressed

E

by a woman speaker, who used somewhat blasphemous language and constantly used our Lord's name as an oath. She told the others of her discomfort, and it was decided that she must go to the promoters of the meeting and make her protest. This she did, and found that they, too, were unhappy about the tone the speaker had adopted. So they wrote to report the matter to the organization which had sent her, and they also wrote to the woman concerned to tell her that while they had agreed with the general purpose of her speech, she had hurt many of her listeners who try to love our Lord by the way she had permitted herself to refer to Him. That is part of what being the "salt of the earth" really means, for salt is purifying and disinfectant. It would have been easier to let it pass in silence. This courageous response to a sudden challenge was naturally a kind of sideline, an uncovenanted chance to bear witness for Christ. The company's common concern was, and still is, an exploration of the relationship between Christianity and physical health.

The third company to be brought under contribution for this miniature anthology started from exactly the same common concern with religion and health as the previous one, but it was led by this interest into a very different field of expression. Their story is the very reverse of a "success story" but it has its glories. The company consisted of some half-dozen people all of whom had been forced by circumstances to think a great deal about the problems of sickness and health, for one of them ran a nursing home, another had endured many years of crippling illness, a third was a masseuse, and all the rest had been forced to live cheek by jowl with sickness at home. So when they came together in an S.C.K. company their concern was ready made for them, though how they should pursue it was by no means so clear. But a string of circumstances brought them into touch with the Peckham Health Centre. They became deeply interested in it and devoted many company meetings to discussing it. Eventually, and rather to their alarm, they found themselves being led into the planning of a vast undertaking. At the time their leader reported it in these words:

We find ourselves embarking on an undertaking for which we feel completely inadequate, yet each step towards it has followed inevitably from the one before. Our concern with health led us to an interest in housing, and to the discovery that it is possible to form a Housing Society which, because it does not trade for commercial profit and pays only a low rate of interest on its shares, can get grants and subsidies for building in the same way as a Local Authority. Any surplus profit goes back into the estate to provide amenities or lower the rents. The Society is now registered, with our Adviser, the Warden, all the members of the company and one other friend as the founder members, and we are organizing a public meeting in November at which we hope to enrol shareholders. What the next step will be is not yet clear, but it is strongly in all our minds that however urgent the immediate need for houses, it is vital to remember that just houses are not enough—they must be grouped and planned to form communities if the people who live in them are to lead a full and satisfying life. Planning for communities would involve building on a fairly large scale, and the company would value tremendously the prayers of S.C.K. in making decisions for the future.

This meeting was held in the Town Hall, and was addressed by two of the pioneers of the Peckham Experiment. Rather to everybody's surprise the hall was full, and those who came were encouraging and enthusiastic. After it was over the company met again and it seemed clear to all its members that they were definitely committed to go further with their housing scheme. They had already formed and registered a Public Utility Society, and they now invited all and sundry to take shares in it. Many did, and soon they had a share capital of over £1,500. Then they appointed a full-time secretary and a consulting architect, and immersed themselves in long and most complicated negotiations for the purchase of land. For what these six people had started had by now become nothing less than a proposal to build an entire housing estate of five hundred mixed-community houses, with a Health Centre in the middle of it. Their scheme was now so big that it had outgrown their own unaided capacity to manage it, and they had to create a new committee of management consisting of men and women with financial and administrative experience.

How delightful it would be if one could only go on to describe how one success led to another, and then point triumphantly to the completed housing estate! But, alas, it did not end like that. One barrier after another came between the company and their desires, and in the event no two bricks were laid on each other.

Had this scheme been launched before the war it might and probably would have succeeded, as many other similar schemes did. But in 1947 it was utterly impossible for any private group of people to build. Only local authorities could get bricks, timber, and glass; only they could command building labour. On the rocks of controls and shortages the scheme finally foundered. The Public Utility Company had to be wound up and the money returned to the shareholders. The failure was not inglorious, but it was sad; and the company picked itself up and went steadily on with its other work. Some people called it Wilful Idealism, and perhaps it was. But it was also an excellent, if a rather grim, example of how easy it is to mistake the guidance of the Holy Spirit, however many safeguards against it you devise. For every single step they took this company had waited upon God, had reached unanimity, and had had their decisions accepted by their adviser. And yet, in spite of all that, the venture had ended in failure.

Another record of achievement comes from a company formed out of the congregation of an artisan parish in South London. The leader himself told the story of how the conception of a full parish conference on evangelism came to them, and where it led them.

I want to tell you of a rather intimidating venture into which we have been led. At a recent waiting upon God which had as its central theme our contribution as a congregation to the conversion of England, we found ourselves agreed on what is, so far as I know, a novel experiment, to which we have given the name of Parish

Conference. We put the plan before the Church Council, which approved it and appointed a committee of seven (three of whom are drawn from the company's five active members) to plan and prepare for the Conference. Briefly the idea is to hold in the autumn a conference of the entire congregation and of any others from the parish who may be willing to attend, and in a series of informal discussion meetings, alternating with prayer and worship, to review the activities of our church one by one, asking ourselves with regard to each: " What does this contribute towards the conversion of this parish and is it the best instrument of its kind that we can offer to the Holy Spirit? " We intend that there shall be a good deal of preliminary publicity, so that people may be induced to read the report of the commission and to think and pray about it. If possible, we want those who are responsible for the conduct of each organization—the Sunday Schools, Scouts, Fellowships, etc.—to prepare a written report, so that copies of these statements may be available before the meeting and the local facts may be in the hands of all who participate. Each meeting would be carefully " reported," so as to gather up findings at a final general meeting, and there would be a standing committee to carry on afterwards, testing out the suggestions made at the conference and carrying them into effect as far as possible.

We think the conference might begin with a corporate communion of the organizers and speakers on a Friday. About 8 p.m. there would be a united service, invoking the guidance of the Holy Spirit and offering the conference. Five or six meetings would follow through Saturday and Sunday, the final meeting being held before Evensong, so that the findings might be offered at the altar at that service.

Strictly speaking, the company as such has no responsibility for this venture, but the idea came to us as a company, and as individuals we are carrying most of the burden. We hope therefore that other companies may be interested in the scheme and that they will keep our parish in their prayers.

All this plan was carried through, and every one of the parish organizations and societies loyally submitted themselves to the kindly questionings of the congregation. In due course this has led to many different evangelistic efforts in the parish. They have ranged from a mission to a novel enterprise of composing and publishing a series of news letters commenting on current events from a Christian point of view, and which members of the company take out to selected families. In fact what is so striking about this company is their astonishing fertility of invention. They have undoubtedly succeeded in establishing in the parish both the idea and the actual fact of the permanent mission.

The last example of what an S.C.K. company may find itself undertaking is a real saga, and in the nature of things a very long one. This is because it is the story of how a particular family in desperate need was helped. Inevitably it has no proper ending, for there is never an end this side of the grave to all the needs of any human family. The story is told by a member of the company, and as anyone will see who reads it, it has been necessary to make quite, quite sure that the reader cannot identify the family concerned. I have therefore ruthlessly suppressed all the names and invented new ones. The scene is a medium-sized English midland town, and the company consists of its leader, a woman social worker, who writes the story, and eight or nine other young men and women.

It seems incredible that we have only known the Brandts for two years, and most of our company would find it difficult to visualize a time when almost the first remark any of us made on meeting one another was "How are the Brandts?" The last two years have presented us with a non-stop series of crises to try to cope with.

The back history, before we came into the picture, is that Elsa Brandt was the eldest daughter of a respectable working-class family in reasonably good circumstances. Early in the war she met a Dutch Naval Petty Officer, Brandt, and married him. From the pictures it was an exceptionally pretty wedding, attended by several officers from Brandt's ship. They had a very comfortable, pleasant little home with one child, Joey. From all accounts they were very happy, and Mrs. Brandt still loves him very much indeed. At the end of the war Brandt returned home to Holland, ostensibly to see his parents. He never returned, and enquiries through the Red Cross revealed that he had married in Holland before the war and had a wife and two children to whom he had returned. Mrs. Brandt was completely broken by this, as she had had no suspicions whatsoever that Brandt was previously married. To make matters worse, her father refused to believe that she was innocent, and forbade her to come to the house. The mother sided with Elsa, and for the first time there was serious friction in the home. Meanwhile, during all the months of uncertainty, Elsa had got into financial difficulties, had to move into rooms in a tenement house and get rid of bits of furniture. Six months after the news of the bigamy her mother died suddenly. Brothers and sisters were scattered and not too sympathetic anyway, and Elsa felt completely alone. She went out to work and tried to bring up Joey decently—spoiling him a good deal in the process. She had no particular religious belief, only a deep sense of guilt.

On New Year's Eve, 1947, the people in the rooms up above invited her to a party they were holding, and there she met Jimmy. They drank a good deal, and as she was not used to it, it went straight to her head, and before she had time to think she found herself in bed with Jimmy. In the morning she felt a bit ashamed, but when Jimmy turned up again a few days later with presents—well, it was nice to have someone to be kind to her, and they drifted into a spasmodic sort of relationship. She wasn't in love with him and never imagined she was. But he was kind and warm and rather pathetic, and above all he needed her. When she found she was going to have a baby, he told her he was married, had a wife and three children, but he never saw them as his wife no longer wanted him, and that he would try to get a divorce and marry her. Before the baby was born Jimmy was off on a job which kept him away from home, and Elsa lived on National Assistance. Jimmy wrote occasionally, and when he returned was delighted by his baby son William. There was a grand reunion, and then Jimmy was off again leaving Elsa to discover she was again pregnant. This time, for some reason, Jimmy did not write, and the months went by. William was barely twelve months when Jeannette arrived. Meanwhile, various officials, deeply shocked by the immorality of the household, had stepped in, given Mrs. Brandt a piece of their mind—told her that she wasn't fit to be the mother of children, and that there would be no more help with clothes, etc., unless she allowed Jeannette to be adopted. Jimmy didn't write, Elsa was undernourished, weak and friendless, and she bowed to the force of their arguments, begging only to be allowed to breast feed the baby for a few weeks to give it a good start. Something about this girl baby captured Mrs. Brandt's heart, and when they finally came to take it away she felt it was more than she could bear. She lost interest in herself and her home, and was very near suicide.

That is the story up to the time that our S.C.K. company came into the picture—I'm sorry to have been so long about it, but it doesn't make sense unless you know the background.

I think the first thing we realized about Mrs. Brandt was that she felt utterly cut off from ordinary human contacts and that she had little idea of how to respond to friendship. I think at first she regarded us as a more benign form of superior interference. She nearly sent us mad by referring to us as "all you kind people from the church," and she obviously regarded us as a species apart and assumed an almost nauseating Uriah Heep kind of attitude which she has now completely outgrown. The first problem, of course, was the baby—she wanted it back so badly, and yet she knew that she had only a life of poverty to offer it, but she grieved incessantly for it. We prayed about it a great deal, and felt that unfair pressure had been brought to bear on her, and that whatever material advantages the child might enjoy in its new home, the love of its own mother was beyond purchase price, and so, after a lot of thought, we advised her to have it back—she had, of course, as yet signed no legal papers for adoption. It was at this point that I realized what strength of character she was capable of showing, for she put up a terrific fight against a number of very forceful officials, and at last won the fight and Jeannette came home. I shall never forget

how radiant she looked on that first evening with the
baby on her knee and William and Joey playing by
the fire. "I've never been so happy in all my life," she
said. "I will try to be good now for the children's
sake."

We rallied round her with clothes for the children and
Christmas gifts, and the next great event was the
christening of the babies. Elsa had never realized that
illegitimate children could be baptized. The Vicar explained it all to her very carefully, and her part in the
Christian upbringing of the children, and some of our
S.C.K. company were God-parents to the children. After
the baptisms we had a party with a christening cake
and presents for all the children and the Vicar for tea!
Snaps were taken of the Vicar and Elsa and the babies,
and Elsa was thrilled and began to feel a bit of self-
assurance and pride in her family. Neighbours began
to be a little more friendly, and occasionally one would
sit with the children so that Elsa could come to church
or I could take her to the pictures. Joey joined the choir
—a not very satisfactory experiment which is a story
in itself and outside the scope of this! All through this
period one tried to build up something like reciprocal
friendship. It was an uphill climb and there was the
tendency for us to be the givers and Elsa the receiver,
which was fatal to any real friendship. Bit by bit I tried
to build up the two-way traffic idea, at one time saying
that after a heavy day's work the least she could do was
to give me a cup of tea, that I, too, had a birthday,
and that a card cost little but meant a lot, and bit by
bit the penny dropped, till last Easter it was Mrs. Brandt
who suggested that we all put an extra 5s. in the Easter
offering so that the Vicar, who was looking desperately
tired, could afford a decent holiday. And she saved
hers! And this year my birthday was celebrated with

a pair of nylons and a bunch of violets. On her income (National Assistance) this is truly sacrificial giving.

Just before Easter 1951, I arrived one day to find that Jimmy had returned. Elsa was looking pretty and excited, and the house was full of gifts for her and for the children. Jimmy was completely overcome by shyness when he saw me, and withdrew to the kitchen. Elsa told me that she had explained to Jimmy that she wanted to bring the children up as Christians, and that she didn't intend to live with him any more, and that he had agreed, but said that there wasn't any harm in him coming to see them all occasionally and her going to the pictures with him. I knew it couldn't rest there. I knew well from the way she held my hand in the pictures the desperate need for affection, and I could see, too, that Jimmy, who was a pathetic type, drew out her maternal instinct as well as her need for affection. I think we were all baffled. The roots of her new-found faith were so shallow as yet. We suggested that she was playing with fire, but she was adamant —she had promised us that she wouldn't ever sleep with Jimmy again, and she wasn't ever going to break it.

After this I often encountered Jimmy, and then she admitted that he had left the Navy and was lodging with her. He was sleeping on the couch in the living-room—but now she was less happy, and there was a barrier between us, and some of her self-assurance had gone. We had a day's outing in the country, and Elsa told me she wished she could get rid of Jimmy. She didn't love him, and wanted him to go back to his wife. He had been violent, too, because she refused him. I asked if we could help, but she thought she could manage, and was diffident about seeing the Vicar. Then

came the summer holidays. I was away for a month
and returned to find Elsa looking ill and wretched.
Jimmy was still there and stayed in the room during
my visit. I felt I was embarrassing them both by my
presence. In October I called again. Elsa was alone this
time, and she told me very coldly not to call again. Her
face was so agonized that I guessed what had happened,
and took her in my arms, where she sobbed out the whole
story. Yes, she was pregnant again, and she had thrown
away the chance she had been given, and now there was
no hope for her. I enquired about what provision was
made. This time she hadn't dared to go to a doctor or
get a nurse. Jimmy had given her no money to get
clothes—the napkins were worn out and so were nearly
all the baby clothes. She hated Jimmy and wanted him
to go, but he was threatening her that if she turned him
out he would tell the National Assistance Board of the
money he had given her, and then she would go to
prison. She implored me not to tell the Vicar. She
could not bear him to know she had failed. I told her
nothing we could ever do would separate us from the
love of God, and that the Church stood ready to receive
her children with loving arms whenever they wished to
return, and that the Vicar would not be less her friend
because she had tried and failed, but I don't think she
believed me at the time. The next day I returned, and
the first question was, "You didn't tell the Vicar, did
you?" "Yes," I said, "and he sent you this with his
love and the message that he would come and see you
soon." As she opened the parcel and found two dozen
new babies' napkins, I think we were both a bit blinded
with tears.

In the next week or two the Vicar and I both visited
several times and became convinced that Elsa really did
want to get rid of Jimmy. She said she had asked him

many times to go, but he flatly refused to do so. Could
we help her? Attempts by us to talk to Jimmy failed as
he was uncommunicative and usually cleared off when we
arrived. The company held council, and it was finally
decided that the Vicar, J.C. (a very large young man)
and I should go to the house, the men to forcibly push
Jimmy out and I to sleep with Elsa in case the shock
of the row brought on a miscarriage or Jimmy returned
in the night. We said our prayers together and set off.
Elsa and the children and I sat in the kitchen while
the Vicar and J.C. dealt with Jimmy in the living-room.
We were all rather scared while we waited, and tried to
hear what the raised voices in the next room were saying.
I wish I could describe the scene in the living-room,
but I can't. After what seemed an age, the Vicar came
into the kitchen and said that Jimmy would go, but
he had no idea where to go and no money for lodgings.
We pooled our resources and managed to raise £1 for
Jimmy, and while the men held the fort and Jimmy
collected his few things, I went off to find digs for him.
Eventually J.C. took Jimmy off to his new digs in the
car, the Vicar went off to a finance committee, and Elsa
and I were left. J.C. had promised to return soon, and
as we had none of us had anything to eat, I got a meal
ready with some stuff we had brought with us, and Elsa
started to get the children to bed. It was then that I
realized, as no amount of visiting could have taught me,
under what inconveniences the very poor live. The
scullery with no light but a small bit of candle stuck
on a broken saucer, the one small cracked enamel basin
in which the family bathed, the nappies were washed,
the washing-up was done and the vegetables were prepared. God knows how they do it and keep reasonably
clean, as Elsa and many others do. To add to the confusion the gas went out and there was a wild searching

for pennies before we could relight the sitting-room light
or heat the water. Somehow we managed, and, the
children in bed, sat down to eat hot sausages out of the
frying-pan, the only plates and knives and forks being
dirty from Jimmy's supper, and the hot water in the
one small kettle having been needed for washing children.
J.C. said he had never enjoyed a supper more, and even
Elsa recovered enough to laugh at the picnic. We were
in fact all enjoying ourselves after the strain when the
door opened and in walked Jimmy. Reasonably enough,
I think he could have killed J.C. and me. He bellowed
that if Elsa wouldn't have him, he wanted everything
he had ever given her, and began with slow deliberate
movements to wrap up a small fancy inkwell on the
mantelpiece. We sat fascinated while we watched him
wrap and unwrap this inkwell into different shaped
parcels. Jimmy, satisfied with the effect he was making,
surveyed us in silence and then hissed, "Watch, cats!"
He left the room, climbed the stairs and then came
down. "I'll have the key of the bedroom, please. I
want the blankets off the kids' beds." Elsa pleaded;
J.C. only just controlled his impulse to knock Jimmy
down; I said, "All right, Jimmy, if they are yours, and
you feel like that, you'd better take them and I'll share
what I've got with Elsa." "I don't want the ——
blankets," he swore, and went off, leaving the inkwell
behind.

A few moments later we heard Jimmy return, and
there was a loud crash as he broke open the bedroom
door. J.C. was up the stairs like a shot, and told me to
fetch the police. When the police came they said it was
a domestic quarrel and they could do nothing, but they
gave Jimmy a piece of their mind and told him not
to return, which advice he ignored three times more that
night. When he finally discovered that his place in bed

was actually filled by my not inconsiderable bulk, he gave it up as a bad job!

The next morning J.C. put a new lock on the door. The next evening we had a repeat performance! And so it went on for several days. Meanwhile we tried to make arrangements for the approaching confinement. Officials were duly shocked by the imminence of a third illegitimate baby. It was time, they said, that Mrs. Brandt was taught a lesson. No, she could *not* have a bed in hospital.

In desperation J.C. and his wife took Jeannette into their home, the church raised money for William to be boarded out in a foster home, and Elsa and Joey spent their nights with me. The Vicar vowed one day that he would get Elsa into hospital if he phoned officials all day. He at last succeeded. Michael, called after the Vicar, was born this year. He is a very beautiful boy, and J.C. and his wife are godparents. S.C.K. companies and friends worked like trojans, and Michael was as well provided for as any little prince.

Jimmy called at my house nearly every evening to ask where Elsa was and if the baby was born. Sometimes he would come in and have a cup of tea, and he became more friendly and communicative. He did love Elsa and wanted to marry her if only he could get a divorce. I tried to explain to him that the best way to show his love was not to ask Elsa to live with him unless he could marry her, and that he ought to try to be reconciled to his wife. He took a poor view of this. He came to church with me on Sundays, wistfully trying to understand what it was that was giving Elsa strength to stand against him. What was this new love that had come into her life? He was as bewildered and wretched as an orphan child, and pathetically grateful for small kindnesses. J.C. and N. and I had him in for a drink on

Christmas morning after church, and then felt bad about sending him off to spend the day alone, but there are certain things you can't thrust on a family. He was generous, too, with the way he brought gifts for the children and Elsa, which he left for me to give them.

The baby had been overdue and Elsa had a long rest in hospital—the first real rest she had had for years. She looked much younger and happier than I had ever seen her, and she was determined by God's help to lead a good life and to bring the children up in the Christian faith. Jimmy came to visit her, but she came to an arrangement with a neighbour next door to come in whenever Jimmy came, so that she was never left alone with him. She went to bed very early, and J.C. reinforced the bedroom door so that it would take a high explosive to knock it down. Jimmy was very chastened and gave very little trouble. He continued to come to church, and we rather sat back and felt at ease.

Mrs. Brandt realized that she knew very little about the Christian religion—she did not know how to teach the children to say their prayers or how to say her own. Such friends and neighbours as she knew would also like to hear. Could we teach them? You will know with what alacrity this request was granted, and now at the point where I should like to say most I shall be able to say least, for I think nothing in my life has moved me as those evenings the Vicar and I spent with Mrs. Brandt and her neighbours, whilst he told them the old, old story, and they heard it in some cases for the first time. It was, as Mrs. Brandt said, " Sometimes as though Jesus Himself walked in and sat round the fire with us."

It was on one of these evenings that we got to know

F

our friend Phyl. I shall never forget her complete incredulity as she asked, "Do you really mean that God *loves* us—even when we've been bad?" Then out tumbled her life story, her unfaithfulness to her husband during the war, how he had left her and she had picked up with one Yank after another. She had four children by three different fathers. She had known that God would punish her, but once you'd sinned like that you might as well go on. Very tenderly the Vicar explained that sin wasn't only breaking the law—it was breaking the heart of God. The next week Phyl wasn't there. She had a headache, she said, and the following week came the same message. Something compelled us to go in. We found our way down the next-door basement in the dark, the last pennyworth of gas was exhausted and Phyl was in bed. The Vicar talked to her for a few minutes, and then we knelt and prayed. Phyl confided in Elsa the next day that the pain left her as the Vicar prayed. She didn't miss another meeting. She, too, had thought that her illegitimate children could not be christened. One of the nicest things that happened for me was when the Vicar entrusted me with the preparation for their baptism. It was a lovely service. Members of our company were godparents, and we had a lovely party afterwards, for which another company provided cakes. Really an S.C.K. do! The one shadow on the proceedings was that Elsa came to the party with a scarf round her neck, and when I questioned her she admitted, showing me the black marks, that Jimmy had tried to strangle her because she refused to sleep with him.

Phyl had been confirmed many years ago as a girl, but hadn't been to church for twenty years and felt she wasn't good enough. Elsa felt that she would like to be confirmed, so our house meetings turned into confirmation classes. Jimmy attended too, saying nothing, but looking vacantly into space, though he was always ready to hand round tea and offer cigarettes. The week before the confirmation Jimmy became very restive and came every evening to see Elsa, begging her, "Don't take them vows, Elsa. I know what it means—you'll never sleep with me no more—I know you won't if you take them vows." He came to church for her first Communion, refused to sit with us, but watched her all the time like a whipped dog. Phyl made her Communion on this day too, and until recently they both came to church on Sunday at some service, helping each other out with the children, and attended the 11 a.m. Communion on Wednesdays.

One Sunday evening late in August, we had all been to Evensong, Phyl, Elsa, Jimmy and I. Phyl and Elsa had been in for a bit of supper with me, and Jimmy had gone back to his digs. All seemed to be flowing calmly when the phone rang and Phyl's eldest girl called, "Please come quickly, Jimmy is trying to murder Mrs. Brandt." I phoned J.C. and got the car out. When I arrived there was Elsa on the front doorstep, semiconscious and covered with blood. Jimmy had said he was staying, so she had run out. When I got inside there was, of course, no sign of Jimmy, and I persuaded Elsa to come in and lie down while I saw what had happened. He had kicked her several times and scratched her face, which accounted for the blood, but there didn't appear to be much in the way of serious damage. Soon after J.C. arrived, sensibly bringing a policeman with him. The policeman searched the house and gardens, but could see no sign of Jimmy. No sooner had they gone than we found him under the kitchen window. He yelled that he'd kill her and all the children if she wouldn't have him back, but he made off before

J.C. could catch him. We fetched the police, and by this time a crowd had gathered and were imagining that Elsa had been murdered. Providentially Elsa's brother passed, and hearing what the commotion was, he came in and made up a quarrel of years, for he had scarcely spoken since the original bigamy was discovered. He said he would take Elsa and all her children to his home —a noble offer as he lived with his father—and that Elsa must bring a charge against Jimmy. She did all this and the family feud is now resolved. Between the issuing of the summons and the case Jimmy got into the house on several occasions, threatening Elsa in my presence with murder. I gave evidence in court and so did Phyl, and Jimmy got off with a warning and a fine of £2, with a month to pay. As we left the court room Jimmy again threatened Elsa, and I felt that he had now got so desperate that he might carry out his threat. The Vicar and I talked and prayed, and felt that we could not let Mrs. Brandt return home alone. There was a limit to how long she could stay with her brother and his wife in their tiny house, and the Vicar flatly forbad me to go back to sleep with her at home. Then we had a brainwave. We would hire a caravan on a remote site and park the whole family there until we could get the housing authorities to do something. Her basement dwelling was barely fit to live in, and in spite of soap and water and disinfectant, which Elsa used with zeal, the place stank and there were bugs in the walls.

So we packed the whole family into cars and off to the caravan for a holiday. One of the other S.C.K. companies produced hampers of food, others lent linen, and Elsa was rigged up in some decent frocks so that she didn't look too different from the other caravan dwellers. They were happily settled, the Vicar turned up, and we all had tea in the caravan and thanked God we could sleep that night without anxiety, and could picture Elsa and the children getting brown by the sea. And so we left them and went home.

Two days later I called. Elsa was lying in a veritable pool of blood, fellow caravaners were fetching the doctor and minding the children. She was again pregnant, and this was a threatened miscarriage. The doctor ordered the ambulance and she was taken to hospital, where she was dangerously ill for some days. I rang the Vicar, who fetched Phyl and her family, and for a week they looked after the Brandt family. Then we applied for the Children's Officer to take them into care, and some of the others took them along to the Children's Home. Through all this period our youngest member took all the dirty washing home, including napkins—an unspectacular but quite heroic job, I think.

The Vicar visited Elsa in hospital, and we are all prepared to accept her statement that this pregnancy is the result of rape. During the long time in hospital we were all impressed by the increase in her spiritual stature. She has no trace of Uriah Heep now, but a quiet dignity and a great gratitude to God and to the Church.

Meanwhile Jimmy, unable to find out where Elsa and the children were, has given it up as a bad job and gone to Scotland, from where he writes pathetic letters sent care of my address.

Elsa came out of hospital, and soon after was given a council house on the outskirts of the town. We are all delighted and she is immensely grateful. One of the members of our Company helped her with all the heavy work of moving and laid the lino, while others provided food for the great day. The Vicar into whose parish she has moved has already visited twice and been most kind and helpful, and though Elsa still wants to keep her connection with our church, we feel she will find at least a second home in her parish church. We are going to have a special little service of thanksgiving and blessing in the house next week.

We hope so much, as does Elsa, that Jimmy will never find her new address if he returns, but somehow I think he will. We have failed with him, of course, and left him bitter and bewildered. It is difficult to see how we can help him, except by prayer. The baby has, of course, been saved, so we still have that to face, and goodness knows how we shall manage, for I expect little help from official quarters. I have already been rung up and more or less told it is my fault that she is pregnant—which sin I repudiate! However, the baby isn't due till the end of February, and God, who has never failed us in our previous troubles, will surely help us with the next.

On such a tale as that, commentary would be an intrusion and praise impertinent. One can only thank God for all this persistent heroism, and for the lesson these people exemplify—that you cannot "love people in Christ" if you refuse to get personally involved in their affairs, and at the earthly material as well as the purely spiritual level.

These five accounts of company activities are, however, exceptional. They constitute the highlights. During these years we never at any one time had less than between fifty and sixty companies up and down the country, and to the great majority of them nothing as spectacular as this happened. They simply "kept on keeping on" with their chronicles of small beer. They set about preparing their parishes for the return of the service men. They raised money for the Church in China or for rehabilitation in Europe. They adopted families of Displaced Persons. They flung themselves into parish missions. They visited lonely old women. They worked away at their concern with health and healing. They were faithful intercessors. They helped young confirmation candidates. On earthly values it all sounded a little pedestrian. Was it for this sort of thing that we had founded S.C.K., they constantly asked themselves, and then they would lay it all before the Holy Spirit in waiting upon God, and the answer would come; "Carry on: no change." In heaven no doubt there was rejoicing, for after all they were all the time transvaluing routine, and that is never a mean feat. But we were not in heaven, and sometimes the word Frustration was too often heard. At one point it became necessary to write a pastoral letter to all the companies to remind them all how essential a virtue patience is for all who are trying to do a really big job in an exclusively spiritual way.

We are trying to fit ourselves to fill a place in the whole Christian line of battle which is at the nerve centre of the line; and therefore it is one of those places at which the real fighting will have to be done. At present we are a set of recruits in training—not more than that—but we are training, for something big with destiny.

The essence of our training is to learn to rely completely upon the power and energy of God, and to do this corporately and in fellowship. This has meant for us all no slight degree of self-control, for if we were to regard ourselves as recruites in training, we could have to think of S.C.K. as an instrument we were learning to handle, and did not know much about. So we could not allow ourselves publicity, and we were bound to move always along the most difficult road of all—a purely spiritual road, which only those can tread who have the very difficult grace of patience. God is never in a hurry, but it is extremely hard for His children of to-day not to be. If they are any use, they are ardent; and if they are ardent, they want to get on. Perhaps it is the chief of the many things for which we have to give thanks, that we have resisted the temptation to take short cuts and to try to rush the growth of S.C.K. by premature battery and assault.

At present we are passing through the first of many difficult phases which must necessarily lie in the path we have to tread. Many companies feel that they have served a long enough apprenticeship of comparative inaction, and they ought to be doing something definite and tangible, but no chance of it seems to come their way. Nearly every company is struggling with that sea of difficulties which these times bring upon us in great waves—people who have less and less time to give; members of companies suddenly snatched away and sent to the ends of the earth; everybody tired, strained, tense; and the likeliest recruits, filled indeed with sympathy, but most hesitant to commit themselves under present circumstances to the kind of discipleship that ours is. Many letters from company leaders, and more personal knowledge of a number of the companies, shows clearly that S.C.K. can no more escape the burden of frustration than can the whole Church. It is indeed for us resolutely to take up our share—perhaps rather more than our share—of this load which presses daily upon every Christian who means business by his religion.

As the Church is the spiritual Body of Christ, it can no more escape from the burden of the Cross than the physical body of Jesus could. But the particular form of the Cross which the Church bears varies from one generation to another, according to circumstances. The cross laid upon our generation of Christians is Frustration. We all desire so passionately to give ourselves to God's service and Man's true need; we are willing to pay the price of sacrifice. Then, over and over again, circumstances and accidents hold us up and keep us back. We must think of it as the particular cross we have to bear. Now the Scripture says that no one can be following Christ who is not bearing a cross. There are many things we can do with crosses, but some of them are not wise. We must not get resigned to the cross we bear, nor become impatient and angry because it is heavy, nor be always complaining because it hurts our shoulders and our backs ache. A cross is given us to bear, and we have to use it as a ladder.

Brave words! But they must have had some effect. For while most companies felt, as they still feel, that their actual record of achievement falls far short of their hopes, and even that this record is really one of "doing nothing in particular," yet very few companies have ever been driven by this to give up the struggle and disband. They have found the high degree of fellowship too valuable to them all for it to be thinkable for them to deprive themselves of it, and they have undoubtedly been helped in this by being kept steadily in touch with all the other companies everywhere else. It showed them that their own story of quite unspectacular perseverance was also the story of many of the others, but that if you added it all together it made a sum total not to be despised, no matter by what standards it was judged.

But in spite of all we could do by conferences, news letters, regional gatherings, visiting, and encouraging the companies to write regularly to each other, it was still true that it was very difficult for any one company to see the whole picture. Only the warden and secretary could really do that. Now though we deal with the companies as corporate units, and though by the rules there is no such thing as an isolated companyless member of S.C.K., a man cannot be warden of it for ten years without gaining a vast amount of knowledge of its individual members, and a great deal of personal pastoral work among many of them comes his way. Having held this office from the beginning, if I were now to be asked to make a list of the positive achievements of S.C.K., I should place very high on the list what under God it has done for its individual members. There is no question about it. People of all kinds and ages, but above all the young, who spend a number of years in one of our companies, who subject themselves faithfully to its disciplines and let themselves gain strength from its fellowship, do grow up in Christ in the most astonishing way. It seems to keep them quick and eager, courteous and loving, and to sharpen and temper all the native spiritual faculties they had to begin with. One of the bishops, who was among the original founders and has been closely in touch with it all ever since, is fond of saying, "The great thing about S.C.K. is not really what it does, but the way in which it seems able to keep all its members 'hotted up,' so

that when their chance to bear their witness does come
—and it generally comes suddenly, like a bolt from the
blue—they seize it at once, and know what to do."
There are many stories I could tell to show how true
this is. It is always rather like the sudden coming to
life of the old promise in the gospels: "The Holy
Spirit shall teach you in that hour what ye shall speak."
For those who have long lived with the others in
intimate touch under His obedience, the promise always
comes true. And the interesting thing is that it seems
to make no difference whether they come from a company which has been given exciting or apparently rather
dull things to do. The growth in the things of the
Spirit comes to them all, and equally to them all.

It is not surprising, therefore, that in these ten years
a steady stream of candidates for ordination and for
various posts in the mission field has passed through
our S.C.K. companies, and at least some found their
vocation in and through their membership of them.
Exact figures do not exist because it has never occurred
to anyone to compile them, but there must be at least
ten young men now ordained who had some part of
their training in one or another of our companies, and
by no means all of them intended to offer themselves
for ordination when they first became members. In
the same period four of our younger members have
found their vocation to the mission field and are now
at work in Africa, India and Malaya; and one or two
others are at present in training in England. In addi-
tion two others have become nuns in a convent.

Personal stories of the growth of individuals cannot
be told here. There are so many of them, and most of

them are confidential. But as a sample here are two spontaneous letters of testimony which I have leave from the writers to quote. The first writes:

> I wish I could tell you the story of how S.C.K. has completely changed my life, of something akin to a miracle which happened as a result of our conference last year, but the story so intimately concerns the lives of some who would mind it being committed to paper that it must remain untold. I can only tell you that through advice given by the Bishop of X, and subsequently followed up by the vicar, no less than five lives have been completely altered, and one of us saved from grievous sin. For myself, S.C.K. has revolutionized my life, giving me an anchorage and peace and security I'd never known before, as well as giving me a purpose in life and leading me into plenty of adventures. I shall never be able to tell you how grateful I am to be allowed to share in the membership.

The other letter was written by a girl who was for some time a member of one of our companies, and then had to pull out because she removed to another part of the country.

> Ever since that time when, as you know, I had a winter of very deep depression and unhappiness—ever since then the only thing that has held me to the Christian faith at all has been the fact that I had been in S.C.K. and had had, especially through its conferences, an experience of Christian community which I just couldn't forget or deny. I think it's beginning to come back, though I've got a fearful amount of prayer and meditation to learn all over again. But when there seemed no

longer to be any contact with God at all, and prayer was quite dead and concentration impossible anyway, I still knew that through S.C.K. I had been made certain of the existence of God; and so I couldn't now just give it all up as I felt strongly inclined to do.

Chapter Seven

THE EVANGELISTIC TENSION

THE next date of importance in the development of S.C.K. was August 1948, for not until then were we relieved of the major uncertainty which had dogged our footsteps ever since the day of our foundation. This uncertainty was really an unresolved dilemma, which was always with us, and at times seemed so formidable as to threaten us with the appearance of semi-paralysis. We were always quite sure of the structural rightness of the shape which S.C.K. had taken, and at no time did we doubt it. But whereas we had built it in the belief that its chief purpose would be directly evangelistic work, and designed it accordingly, this seemed so seldom to be the actual use to which it was put. The companies were doing every kind of excellent work, except for the one work which we had supposed they would nearly all be called to do. They were doing wonderful things in the pastoral sphere, but for the most part they did not seem to be very militant evangelists. At bottom, this was the old tension which every generation of Christians has to solve. If you are an ardent, militant Christian, determined to convert the world, is it better for you to work within and upon the existing Christian community and try to make it more like the Body of Christ, or should you go straight for the world of the factory and the mine and make that secular world your direct target? Of this tension or dilemma we had become increasingly conscious, and we viewed it with mounting discomfort. It had gradually become for us a problem which we seemed able neither to solve nor to let alone, until at last, as the next chapter will show, it was resolved for us in a way which looked so accidental that none of us could possibly have expected it.

On the one hand, it was for evangelism that we had created S.C.K. Its structure was built up with the idea that the purpose of all our companies would be to work directly for the conversion of England, or of wherever else in the world they might form, as for example, one did form and work in China, and, I believe, works there still, though no news comes from them now, nor dare I write to them. At the opening conference we were always using words and phrases like The Permeation of the Natural Communities of the Secular World, or Infiltrating into the Factories and the Mines. The conception was that little by little an S.C.K. company composed of churchpeople employed there should be planted in every factory, every regiment, every institution, such as the B.B.C., the great Trades Unions, and even the House of Commons. We were always being told how desperately urgent this was, and well-wishers used to impress on us in grave tones how exceedingly important was the work to which we had set our hands.

We had, therefore, been specially careful to make S.C.K. very simple and absolutely flexible in its organization; and one reason for the No Publicity rule was that the kind of infiltration we had in mind would be hampered from the start if it has been advertised openly. We had created two types of company, the parochial company to work within the parish congregation and the vocational company to work in the world outside. But all our hopes were set on the latter, and we had supposed that for every parochial company we should have twenty vocational companies. But in the event it worked the other way round. For every vocational company there were twenty parochial companies. The companies which did arise from within the secular world were nearly all of them composed of men or women in the Forces, and when the war ended they naturally ended too. There was indeed one company formed in a big factory, but circumstances which it never had the slightest chance of controlling quickly overwhelmed it, and it perished long before it had any opportunity to do any directly evangelistic work. On the other hand, the companies which were formed out of members of a worshipping congregation always had a steadiness and an air of permanence about them, and nearly all the evangelistic work done by S.C.K. was done by them. It was all very puzzling, and there were times when one surveyed the steady growth of S.C.K. with as much bewilderment as joy, and when one was tempted to exclaim, "It is all a tremendous joy—but it really isn't quite what we meant."

What we had to find out, however, was not so much what we ourselves had meant at the beginning or at any time since then, but what the Holy Spirit meant, for we were there to do His will. S.C.K. consisted of a series of tiny communities whose first purpose was to offer themselves for God to use in whatever way He chose to use them, and this was just as true of the whole body. Indeed it was the basic and fundamental purpose of the whole conception. Moreover we had in the rhythm of waiting upon God a way—the best possible way for frail and faulty human beings —of trying to discover what the will of God for us might be.

So in one conference after another we addressed ourselves to this problem. We must have devoted at least four or five to it alone. We had set out to produce S.C.K. companies in all kinds of secular communities, and we had not done so. We had not set out to produce S.C.K. companies in all kinds of already Christian communities and we had done so. Was this a failure? And if so, what had made it a failure, and could it be put right? Or was this the will of God over-ruling our human desires? That was the crux of the matter for us. From the first it had been a vital principle that prayer and some assurance of the authority of the Holy Spirit must be the condition of all action. So what we had to discover was not whether it was a good thing to produce Christian cells in factories, for that was self-evident, but whether we were ourselves called on to do it, or whether this glory was reserved in the providence of God for some other fellowship.

Only very gradually were we able to come to a decision. There were so many other choices which governed the main choice which had to be dealt with first. For example, it did not take long to become convinced that one reason why it seemed so impossibly difficult to get S.C.K. companies started in factories, and why such as did start never seemed to last, was

G

the fact that we were exclusively a body of Anglican communicants, whereas everybody who knew the inside of factories was sure that anything done there must be done on an undenominational basis. If we were to have more than a very few S.C.K. companies in factories, we should have to forsake our Anglican basis and become an interdenominational fellowship. We could never convince ourselves that it would be right to do this because we were all determined to build S.C.K. on a sacramental foundation. Then there was the tension between Being and Doing. If the quality of company life was what it should be, did it matter so very much what they did? If they were given either heroic or seemingly pedestrian tasks to perform and did them faithfully and well, did it matter so much what they were? The danger of the one attitude was quietism and of the other the heresy that energy will cloak sin and cause it not to matter. It all sounds very simple now, and it is easy to say that it is not a matter of Either—Or but of Both—And, but in the new context in which we were learning to handle a new instrument it never seemed quite so easy as that. We had to arrive at the synthesis experimentally, and it took a great deal of prayer and discussion to do it.

And this new instrument we believed that we were called by God to perfect and to handle, what was it for? It was for evangelism—but, then, what was that? Here, I think, was the root of our confusions. We were not alone in this. That most dubious word confuses practically everybody who uses it, though, alas, it is crying for the moon to ask that it be forthwith deleted from the Church's vocabulary. Is evangelism the effort made by the faithful to convert the unfaithful? If so, most of what our companies had so far been led to do was not evangelistic. Or is it the work of loving people into the Kingdom of God, in which case all the companies could be brought under the definition? Is evangelism the name you reserve to describe the relationship of Christian with absolutely heathen, or does it include the effort to work upon and within the Church to make it care more for those outside the Church and prepare itself the better to receive them when at last they turn again? There was no end to the confusions which this wretched word had caused us. But they can be neatly summarized in the actual experience of one company. It consisted of half a dozen working girls who, after waiting upon God, believed that His will for them was the visiting and befriending of lonely and sick old people. So they went happily to this work and gave up many, many hours of their free time to it. They were of tremendous help to these old people. They met their needs as well as they could, they became their friends, but they made no particular attempt to " convert " them. Then someone who ought to have known better told them that this was not evangelism but just social service, and for some time they were really distressed. Whether technically " evangelistic " or not, it was God's work, done, as they believed, at His bidding, and manifestly what our Lord would approve; and whether it produced " conversions " was no particular business of theirs.

Now if the basic principle of an organization is to begin dealing with every problem by referring it to the

Holy Spirit, and if its guiding principle is to accept no conclusion until it can say that it does so "because it seems good to the Holy Ghost and to us," then plainly you must accept the conclusion you get. If it has been preceded by waiting upon God with all its prayer, discussion and safeguards, and then a unanimous conclusion emerges, it must be treated as a divine order. And if, having returned to the problem again and again, you nevertheless always get the same answer, it becomes faithless to doubt it or even to question it any more. This is what happened to us.

It was at a whole week's conference at St. Swithun's School, Winchester, in August 1948, that we finally "had it all out." There was time to give this dilemma the most searching examination. We split the problem into sections, and gave each section to a small group to consider. Then, in the evenings, these groups came together and compared notes. Thus we prayed and worked for a week, and once more the verdict was unequivocal and unanimous. It was that our history had declared the will of God for us, which was that while any S.C.K. companies which might form in factories or other secular spheres were indeed to be welcomed and rejoiced over, yet our chief function was to work within the framework of the Church. This time we had no right to doubt any more. We had asked the Holy Spirit to show us the right path, and we had used our reason about the dilemma to the utmost possible extent, and in conditions which were ideal for the purpose and gave us plenty of time. After that it would be faithless to doubt any more. Nor have we ever done so since then. There have been plenty of other difficulties, but this long tension had been resolved, and our minds were at ease.

It still remained to find the appropriate form of words to register and make known the decision to which we had at last come. At that time the Lambeth Conference was finishing its sessions, and it was known that it intended to compose a pastoral letter to be read aloud in every Anglican church in the world on a particular Sunday. There was much speculation both on what the bishops would say and whether the language of their letter would be worthy of the occasion, as in fact it was. Pastoral letters were in the air just then, and we thought it would be a good idea if we produced one of our own. So one member of the conference set to work and tried to record its decisions in this apparently easy but actually difficult form. Eventually he produced a draft, and read it to the whole conference. Naturally whatever was sent out must have the authority of unanimous approval of its every word. It meant taking and examining it sentence by sentence, hearkening to the criticisms of sixty people, and finding words and phrases which all could unreservedly accept. To do it took a whole morning, and very few sentences remained exactly as they had at first been written. But in the end the document was greatly improved by this mass scrutiny, and I know of no other assembly of sixty people which could have attempted it without at best ruining it and at worst producing only chaos. Since this document did register the final resolution of our dilemma, and in a real sense constituted our new marching orders, this chapter may fitly end by reproducing at least the relevant parts of it.

THE SERVANTS OF CHRIST THE KING

A letter from the conference at
St. Swithun's School, Winchester, 4th-11th August, 1948
to all Companies and Advisers

———————

The conference of the Servants of Christ the King, gathered at St. Swithun's School, Winchester, from August 4th to 11th, 1948, and consisting of sixty-five representative members of S.C.K. with their Advisers, the deputy Visitor, and other members of the Church, and being, according to our rules, the only governing body of S.C.K., sends this letter to carry its greetings to every company, and asks that it be read aloud at the next company meeting.

We were asked at this conference to discover why nearly all our companies during the last five years had arisen within communities of the wholly or partially converted, and how we might more effectively penetrate the secular communities without doing violence to S.C.K.'s essential principles. To this we applied ourselves for five days of prayer and discussion, and we record the following unanimous convictions about it, which we hope and believe are the leading of the Holy Spirit for us.

While deeply and urgently convinced of the need that we should turn our prayers and activities into the carrying of the Gospel to those who are living contentedly without God in the world, we nevertheless are sure that the first mission of S.C.K. is within the Church. This we believe because the demands of membership in an

S.C.K. company are such that they can be met only by those who are already regular and praying members of the Church, and living its full sacramental life. We are sure we must not weaken those demands, nor forsake our Anglican basis. If this, our conviction, is true, it follows that while we welcome gladly every kind of vocational company, our chief aim at present must be to increase the number of the parochial companies and to use them where possible as a step to the formation of vocational companies.

In order to do this we believe that the No Publicity rule, as it stands at present, must be modified, and we have revised it as follows:

> S.C.K. is a handmaid of the Church which works mostly under the surface of the life of Church and nation. From the beginning it has avoided publicity as far as has been consistent with its normal development and expansion. On the other hand every member is urged to do what he can to spread both S.C.K. and its principles, and may use such methods as do not conflict with the general spirit of the movement.

This we hope will set our hands free without doing violence to the principles which the previous No Publicity rule was framed to guard.

But this extension in the number of parochial companies and the planting of them where they are most needed cannot be accomplished unless we can carry the general body of the parochial clergy with us, and in the past, as we are well aware, we have conspicuously failed to do this. It is a failure on our part to convince them that a company in a parish which rules its life by S.C.K. principles cannot be other than a tower of strength to the parish priest. We therefore call the whole body of S.C.K., and especially its advisers, to do all we can to convince the clergy that S.C.K. is not just another organization, and that they would in fact be enormously helped in their work by it. This we must do in a spirit of sympathy with them in their heavy pressure of work and appreciation of the consistent faithfulness with which they discharge it.

But while we have been thus led to affirm that our primary field of corporate witness is within the Church, we have been led also to a renewed and quickened sense of the urgency of the winning for Christ of all those who are living in forgetfulness of Him, and of the communities and environments in which they are found. We believe, however, that an undenominational cell of a very simple kind will usually be the best instrument for evangelism in a secular community, such as a factory; and we suggest that wherever possible some member of an S.C.K. company should be asked to form such a cell wherever there seems to be an opportunity, while the company supports its ambassador in every possible way and gives to the cell all the help it can both by its prayers and in other ways. We call special attention to two such fields. The first is the whole field of educational work among children, in which so many of our S.C.K. members are already engaged. The second is the whole range of vocational professions and callings, such as medicine, nursing, the magistracy, personnel management and social work generally, where increasing secularization threatens to exclude Christian principles from fields where they are specially vital in order to secure respect for individual personality. It would be a fine thing if these professions were increasingly recruited from convinced Christians, and we should like to see the needs of such callings and the methods of entry to them brought vividly before the younger members of S.C.K.

In all our discussions, moreover, we have continually been reminded of our need of a greater sensitiveness in all our relationships with the people we meet. One group expressed it thus:

> If a company is to be an effective instrument for evangelism its members must be as articulate and sensitive in their dealings with people outside the company as they are with each other. The fellowship we gain from these conferences and retreats, and from our normal company life, should play a large part in developing this articulate and sensitive quality.

We must always remember to think of persons first as persons and not primarily as members of a social milieu or of a vocation or class or even an ecclesiastical group. For so it is that our Lord thinks of us. It is true that we are called to make corporate penetration into the communal groupings which constitute the environment of so many we wish to win. But it is true also that this penetration will only become an embassage of Christ if we are first of all sensitively courteous to the individual personality. Within S.C.K. we do this instinctively and we must learn to do it also outside, and this is our first evangelistic lesson. It is only in the power of steady and imaginative intercession that we may hope to achieve it, and to a renewed effort in such intercession we call each and every company.

Finally, in the peace and great happiness of these days which we have shared together at Winchester (and for which we thank God), we have been convinced that the field of work and witness which S.C.K. is specially equipped to occupy is steadily enlarging itself. We are convinced that S.C.K. must now deliberately set itself to claim more and more of that field. Our principles, our basis of membership, our experience of corporate

joy, remain unchanged, rather our convictions about
these have been deepened by this conference. We have
indicated the ways in which we humbly believe we have
been given to seek to occupy that vast field. We now,
as the only governing body of S.C.K., call upon every
company and every member of S.C.K. to make deliberate
efforts to go forward in Christ's name, and in the spirit
of the Charge given to every one of us on our admission:
"Go forth into the world of men with the Word of God
in your hearts; be witnesses of that Word; speak of it
with boldness; share it with eagerness; convert the un-
believer; recall the lapsed; strengthen the faithful; and
the Blessing of God Almighty, the Father, the Son and
the Holy Ghost, be upon you and upon all the work
you do in His Name and for His glory," and the peace
of the Lord be always with you.

Everything which has happened since then has shown
that this was the right decision; and once we had made
it we were shown in ways that we had not looked for
and which the next chapter describes, that all the time
the dilemma had been unreal.

Chapter Eight

THE TEST CASE OF IPSWICH

FROM the beginning "anonymity wherever possible" has been not a binding rule but an accepted principle of S.C.K. In this book the tradition of anonymity has hitherto been followed as closely as possible, but the history of S.C.K. in the town of Ipswich cannot possibly be told in impersonal and anonymous terms. Any attempt to cloak the story by inventing imaginary names would be quite unreal. What follows, then, is the story of S.C.K. in Ipswich.

Canon R. H. Babington, the Vicar of St. Mary-le-Tower, Ipswich, was one of the original founders. At the time when S.C.K. was still an idea in a very few minds, he was a vicar in the diocese of Winchester, and being less then twelve miles away from me, I kept him in touch with everything which was going on, and continually discussed with him, more than with anyone else, every problem as it arose. He was always a wholehearted supporter and a tower of strength. He left Southampton and went to Ipswich just as S.C.K. was being finally born, and so it was natural that one or two of the earliest companies should form within his Ipswich congregation. One of them, which still exists, was composed of housewives and mothers of young children, and had as its concern the religious training of the very young, and as its expression work the care of the children during the parish Eucharist. The other company consisted of students and young men and women from the services. For a long time there were no other companies there, and so far there was nothing to distinguish Ipswich from half a dozen other towns, such as Bristol, Rugby and Winchester, all of which had rather more companies than Ipswich.

It was soon after the St. Swithun's conference which had set itself to answer the problems described in the last chapter that the new phase in the history of S.C.K. in Ipswich began. It proved to be so important that it can rightly be said to have opened a new chapter in the growth and development of S.C.K. as a whole. Canon Babington called a meeting of all the clergy of the district, and each of them was asked to bring with him two or three of his likeliest lay people. I went to put the case for S.C.K. before them. The meeting was a crowded one, but at the time it didn't seem any more remarkable for enthusiasm than plenty of similar meetings elsewhere, and to this day I cannot for the life of me remember anything that I said. Nevertheless out of all the many scores of meetings that I have addressed about S.C.K., this one bore by far the greatest weight of fruit. There was not, so far as I remember, very much discussion, but before it ended Canon Babington asked any clergy who might be interested to meet him again on a given day and to discuss what might be done to carry it further.

The result of this meeting was the formation of a small company of clergy. At first there were only three of them, Canon Babington and two others, but they refused to be dismayed by this, arguing that if they went forward in faith others would presently ask to join them. So it proved to be. The three soon became six, then nine, and still the company grew. To-day there are two companies of them. About half of them come from the town of Ipswich, and the rest from the villages and little market towns round about. They meet for a whole morning every month, starting with Holy Communion at eight o'clock and continuing until noon; and their rule is that this meeting is of absolute obligation to them all, and nothing whatever is allowed to interfere with it. Knowing one another to begin with, it did not take them long to grow together to the point where their mutual trust and reliance were such that they could truly be said to belong to each other. Very soon it became a matter of second nature to them that any parochial problem on the mind of any one of them was brought to the judgment of all the others before it was decided. From there it was an easy step forward to the position where their separate responsibilities were so fused together by regular prayer and discussion that all their work, wherever it was done, was seen to be one work, an indivisible whole to be planned by the company, acting corporately. Any one of them would say, and in fact has constantly said, that this togetherness in Christ has made the whole difference to their ministry and enriched every single part of it.

Their common concern was fairly clear from the beginning, and they had no great difficulty in identifying it as the growth of the Kingdom of God in the neighbourhood. This they further defined as the need to explore the idea and create the structure of the Permanent Mission. They realized that the conversion of a whole neighbourhood could only be envisaged as an operation lasting for at least a hundred years within which special and particular efforts, such as a mission in this parish or that, would be no more than episodes. The whole operation would be kept moving by a whole series of just such episodes, and one function of the company would be not only to invent them but to link them together in a series so that the second episode reaped the fruits of the first, and the third of the second, and so on continually, until long after all of them had been gathered to their fathers. Important as it was that these episodes within the permanent mission should be rightly conceived and timed, it was more important by far that they should create the structure of the permanent mission, and get the idea of it accepted by all their people as being the normal and regular and not the occasional and temporary condition of the life of the Church.

How they did it will come to be described presently. We turn aside here for a moment to take note of the creative novelties of their action. First, they had begun with the clergy. This was a departure from the normal S.C.K. order which had always been to begin with the lay companies, and only then to hope to combine their advisers into a company of clergy. Their record shows that in this innovation they were profoundly and brilliantly right. As things are in the Church of England you cannot move far without the clergy, and you cannot move at all in opposition to them. It is much better to let them set the pace from the beginning.

Secondly, the fact that a good proportion of the clergy of a neighbourhood had come permanently together on this basis and were doing all their work as a team, made it possible for the evangelistic work of the Church to be conceived and planned on a neighbourhood and not on a parochial basis. This did not in any way deny the separate independence of each parish concerned because all these clergy were parish priests, but it meant that there would be such a fusion of congregations that the concern of one parish was bound gradually to become the concern of them all. Because the clergy had become a team their congregations would tend to become a team too. Separate parishes would remain, but parochialism would gradually die. This has now happened. It is now accepted as the normal condition of affairs in Ipswich that the adventure of one parish is the adventure of all. If St. Polycarp's has a mission, the people from the other parishes come and help as a matter of course, and nobody thinks it specially remarkable. Thirdly, by beginning with the clergy they automatically ensured a steady supply of trained advisers for any lay S.C.K. companies which might form. Thus they solved at one stroke the chronic difficulty, which has dogged us from the beginning, of finding the right clergy to be the advisers of lay companies.

This was particularly important, for if they were to establish the idea and the fact of the permanent mission on a neighbourhood basis, and if the full resources of all the congregations concerned were to be brought into play, they would have to begin by creating within these congregations a goodly number of S.C.K. companies. The witness of the New Testament and the whole history of the Church here were perfectly plain. To vitalize the mass you must first create the leaven, and that means the calling out of the congregation special groups of people to become the trained spearheads of the permanent mission. Bit by bit, therefore, the clergy company began to create new lay companies in many of the parishes they represented. To-day there are ten lay S.C.K. companies in the neighbourhood. Each one of them works on exactly the same lines as any other company. They are separate and autonomous entities. They work out their own destinies. Each one discovers and pursues its own common concern. One runs a large youth club. Another specializes in social ambulance work. A third struggles to improve Sunday Schools. Others do all kinds of parish jobs. All the time they are training themselves in prayer and in religious knowledge, and all the time their devotion is being deepened and their evangelistic sensitiveness is quickened. Over and above their separate concerns is their wider concern with the permanent mission to the neighbourhood. But the planning of this is the business of the clergy company. Under the guidance of the Holy Spirit they decide what is to be attempted next, and they know what they attempt they can actually perform because they have at their command a quite large body of highly trained lay people in the members of the various lay companies, on which they can call whenever it seems necessary and in any way that seems appropriate. Correspondingly, any of the lay companies are perfectly entitled to call on the clergy company for help, and they sometimes do so. In fact they all play into each other's hands. One instance of this is the device of the House Coffee Party, which originated with one of the lay companies, and which has been copied by some of the others and developed into a fine art. The hostess invites eight or nine friends to coffee in the evening. The invitations state plainly that the purpose is to give the guests a chance to ask any questions they like about religion, and to get to know the clergy as friends and not merely as distant figures at the altar or in the pulpit. One of the members of the parsons' company, therefore, is always present. There are now a good many of these House Coffee Parties every month, and they form an excellent bridge between the two worlds which it is the evangelist's business to reconcile. Thus S.C.K. has created in Ipswich a large, varied, trained and highly adaptable body of people which can, so to say, be mobilized at a moment's notice and concentrated upon any piece of work for the growth of the Kingdom of God which needs more resources than any single company could command.

No sooner was this evangelistic instrument created and the idea of the permanent mission accepted, than all kinds of opportunities were offered to it. The Holy Spirit used it to the full; and because all decisions for action are arrived at by waiting upon God for them, this sentence is not presumptuous. The first adventure in which they shared was originated by the whole body of the Ipswich clergy, who concentrated all their resources upon a single large housing estate parish whose vicar was a member of the clergy company. In the summer a hundred and thirty lay people spent every

H

evening for a whole week in intensively visiting all the families in the parish. They were met with kindness and welcome everywhere. There was little or no hostility. Some people were brought into the Church by the visiting, and the visitors themselves gained a new sense of unity and a new conception of the scale of their mission in the England of to-day. It was a sighting shot, not more than that, but it revealed the fact that only a very long-term operation would make much real difference to that or to any other parish.

The next step was taken with this experience behind it. The clergy company began to organize in one parish after another services of witness the aim of which was not so much to convert unbelievers as to recruit new members of the congregation. These services were always addressed by two lay people and one clergyman. At one of them the addresses were given by a schoolmaster and a doctor, and a brief description of another was written in a letter by someone present at it.

The church was packed to the doors and extra chairs had to be brought in. People left the harvesting to come. All the S.C.K. companies were there in force. Needless to say G.W. was at the organ. Can there be an S.C.K. occasion in the Three Kingdoms without G.W. at the organ or the piano? The first talk by a young layman was grand. Then after another hymn came the second talk by a girl in a factory on " Monday to Friday Christian Witness on the Job ". A great many cards pledging people to the Rule of Life suggested by the Lambeth Conference have been taken, and we are snowed under by requests for more. And what next? Our parsons' company meets soon to find out the answer. The interesting thing about S.C.K. is that it lands you in all sorts of adventures and situations which you never really expected.

Thus one by one, the various parish churches of the neighbourhood were strengthened, and their people were taught to work together. A little later on, when one of them embarked on a mission, the visiting was done by a vast army of people who came from all the parishes round about.

But—what next? The last sentence of that letter was now to come true in a rather startling way, and to fling these clergymen into a novel situation which they had certainly never envisaged when they began. It came about like this. One of them, the vicar of a village, met his inn-keeper in the road one day, and was suddenly challenged by him, "Why don't you come into my pub and say to the people there all the things you say in sermons in the church? You parsons should come and talk to the ordinary man on his own ground, and that's in my pub." "Right," said the vicar with alacrity, "I will." But first he went back to his company and laid the challenge before them. They agreed that this chance must not be missed, but that the taking of it must be a corporate work of the company, and not the sole concern of the vicar. So they appointed five others to go with him, and they laid down certain rules to guide their procedure. They were going to the pubs as priests, and therefore they would wear cassocks. They were going to meet the people on their own ground as friends, and therefore they must not preach sermons or make speeches but must listen as much as they talked. Their purpose, therefore, must be to make friends by answering questions. It was this venture which caught the imagination of the world, and led them to a measure of fame, with pictures in the local press, and even, much to their embarrassment, in the *Daily Mirror*. For it turned out to be one of those things which were an immediate success from every point of view. The pub that night was packed, and the takings in the till were more than doubled. New friendships were established, and afterwards cultivated. Soon they were swamped by invitations from other publicans, and ever since then they have visited one pub a month. The team varies its numbers from three to twelve.

On one occasion I went with them to a village pub some eight miles out in the country. The bar was packed with people, most of them from the village, but also there were a number of members of S.C.K. companies who had come out to support their clergy. Our welcome was unmistakable and sincere. We had a lay chairman (this is most necessary), and for three solid hours we simply answered people's questions, and if they desired it, let them contradict our answers and argue. The questions were most of them of the order of "Has science knocked out God?" and "Why are there so many hypocrites in the Church?", but they were genuinely on people's minds, and so it was good that they should be asked and answered in an atmosphere which could never (and should never) have been that of the parish church. If there was a good deal of ignorance, and more prejudice and misunderstanding, there was absolutely no hostility. Nobody made the least effort to score debating points or to make anyone else look silly and ignorant. Not a soul was ever made impatient. We were friends before we began and friends when we ended, a little weary, at 10.30. This atmosphere of a welcoming friendship in every public house which the clergy have visited has puzzled some of them a little. I remember one of them saying at a company meeting, "Why has nobody ever said to us, 'What the so-and-so are these flaming parsons barging in here for?' I think we ought to be going somewhere where they will."

A year or more of this regular public house visitation began to produce evangelistic fruits, but still the company was conscious that there were multitudes of people who were still untouched by the Christian message. Particularly was this true of the men and women working in the factories and heavy engineering works. So they next turned to consider what their company could do to meet this need. They called this their Sons of Toil problem, and their first insight was to realize that they would need to learn a great deal themselves before they could hope fruitfully to tackle anything so difficult. So they put themselves to school by inviting foremen and shop stewards to come and tell them frankly what they thought of the Church, and what they thought the Church ought to be trying to give to the people whom they represented. All this is going on now, and what will come of it remains to be seen since the narrative has at this point overtaken the present day. But that they will find some fresh and inventive way of tackling the most difficult and baffling problem on earth no one who knows the history of the company can doubt.

All this shows plainly that to the Church in Ipswich the phrase, The Permanent Neighbourhood Mission, is one which not only is understood, but describes something which has been accepted and is in being. It would be both presumptuous and untrue to claim that S.C.K. had done it all, for it is in fact a work of the whole Church. But it is true to say that without the S.C.K. companies there it would not have happened. They have been the spearhead of thought and action from the beginning. As this work advances it will probably become difficult to tell which part of it was done by the S.C.K. companies and which by the various congregations as a whole. This is exactly as it should be, for S.C.K. is a handmaid of the Church and not a substitute for it. Their newest venture, the re-opening of Leiston Abbey by a group of Christian people and the equipping and running of it as a diocesan centre of evangelism, is a case in point. It is a diocesan venture which the S.C.K. companies could not possibly have tackled by themselves, but which certainly would not have been tackled without them.

Thus by starting at the right end, with the clergy, and by thinking on the right scale, with the neighbourhood rather than the parish as the unit of power, the dilemma of the choice between whether to work for the Kingdom from within the congregation or by deliberate attempts to infiltrate into the communities of the secular world has never seemed to be relevant in Ipswich. They have demonstrated that the dilemma which seemed so formidable does not really exist, and in this they have shown, too, what the true line of advance is likely to be everywhere else.

Chapter Nine

THE PRESENT AND THE FUTURE

THERE has never been a moment in the history of S.C.K. when any of us thought that the fellowship was a substitute for the Church, and there has never been a conference of S.C.K. in which somebody did not forcefully remind us that we were not the Church. The usual form of this reminder was, "The Church is immortal, but S.C.K. will have its day and then cease to be." It is certainly true, and we have not forgotten it. But this truth, endlessly repeated, is the very stuff of the whole history of the Church. Every branch of the Church in every generation gives birth to a bewildering array of societies, fellowships, guilds, movements, and orders, and while they last they seem to be entrusted with a very large part of the executive work of the Church as a whole. Where, for instance, would the great nineteenth-century missionary expansion of the Anglican Church have been without the missionary societies? It would still not even have begun.

The different movements and societies which arise from time to time within the Church are born, as they would all claim, by the inspiration of the Holy Spirit. They have as their purpose either the performing of some piece of work which the Church is either not doing at all or doing on too small a scale, or else the providing of a visible body to express certain truths and insights of the Gospel which the official Church of the day seems to be heeding too little. Most of them, in fact, try to fulfil both these functions at once, but it makes a good deal of difference which of the two is put first, to be something or to do something. Often, indeed, a movement will begin by setting itself to fulfil one of these purposes; after a time it will change its emphasis from the first to the second; and then in due course change back again to the first. Something of this rhythm is clearly discernible in the history of S.C.K. We began by thinking of it as a means of taking the Gospel to the communities of the secular world. After a time and for a number of years we were led to give far more attention to what we were becoming than to what we were evangelistically achieving. Then in the last two years our thoughts have swung back again to consider what is the particular contribution we ought to be making to the growth of the Kingdom of God.

In 1943, when we began, no idea of filling up that which was lacking in the life of the Church played any part in our minds. We were thinking of evangelism and of little else. Experience shows that this rigid exclusiveness of aim is a passport to early death. If S.C.K. has endured till now, it is because it did produce as it went along certain features in the structure of its organization and the life of its companies which, though certainly prominent in the Holy Scriptures and the Early Church, had been rather overlaid and hidden in the life of the modern Church of England.

The first of these was Waiting upon God. By making it part of the discipline of every company, S.C.K. had become a living, visible, and verifiable example of the ideas about the relationship between God and man through the Holy Spirit which lay behind it. God is energy as well as love, and His wisdom and power are communicated to us when we lay ourselves open to receive them together in expectant dependence and in absolute equality. Waiting upon God does express this, and the proceedings of most ecclesiastical committees seem almost to deny it. This no doubt is why the method of conducting a committee's business by waiting upon God has spread far and wide, so that to-day many bodies are regularly using it, who have never heard of S.C.K. Nor, of course, do we claim any patent rights in it. A great deal of it has been taken over and adapted from the centuries-old procedure of the Society of Friends, and we ourselves inherited it from members of more than one group which had been practising it long before. But it is scriptural through and through and its philosophy is one which the Church of to-day possesses, has largely forgotten, and urgently needs to recover.

Secondly, in an age which fairly revels in excessive complication of organization, in the cords of which the Church itself is almost as enmeshed as the state, S.C.K. is extraordinarily simple and uncomplicated. It has its companies, each one of which leads its own independent life. So long as each one is obedient to the very few and very simple rules no one has the power to give them orders. They do what seems good to them and the Holy Ghost, and if this does not fit into and even contradicts the pattern made by the activities of the other companies round about (as when during a General

Election one company were sure, after waiting upon God, that they should openly help the Commonwealth candidate, and did so) then there is nothing to be done but accept it. S.C.K. is, in fact, organizationally untidy. There are no committees, no subscriptions, no property, and none of the cumbersome apparatus by which so many societies seek to maintain their life. Its only authority is the annual conference of its own members.

A third feature in the structure of S.C.K. which seems to have something to teach the Church is the relationship of the priest-adviser to his company. The word Adviser was carefully chosen and it means exactly what it says. He is not a member of the company and not their leader. He does not attend the meetings by any right of office, but only by their invitation and consent. But he can veto any decision that they make, and anything like a corporate rule of life must have his agreement before it is operative. On the company's side, they have a right to call upon him for any help they need. The relationship is not wholly an easy one, and it does not always work as it should. But it often does, and then it seems as though the ancient and modern problem of the Church of getting the relationship of the clergy and laity right has been at last solved. For if he goes to a meeting of his S.C.K. company the adviser is bound to do a great deal of listening and to hear his people speak with a freedom which they do not ordinarily exhibit before him. The mere fact that they have prayed together and that he has not been in charge of this devotion makes it possible to speak the truth in love. On the other hand just because he is a priest and their adviser he has an authority higher than theirs. If need be, he can veto their decisions and they cannot veto his. In the Church the clergy and the laity are two different orders, each one with its own functions. But neither of these two functions can fully do its work in isolation : it must be supplemented by the other. Half the effectiveness of the Church consists in keeping the functions of priest and layman distinct, and yet joined together in unity and love. S.C.K. does provide a mould within which it is comparatively easy for priest and people to come into the kind of relationship with each other that the Gospel seems to intend.

But if S.C.K. is only a part, one of the lowlier handmaids of the Church, so it is a part and not the whole of the Cell Movement generally. Cells have existed down all the ages of Church history, though only within our own time have they been called by that name. There were plenty of cells in the Church long before S.C.K. was ever thought of, and no doubt there are still. One of the difficulties is that no one knows or can know how many, or where they are, for no register of them exists. More recently the theologians have taken to investigating the idea of the Household Church as it was in the first three hundred years of the Christian era, and trying to find the way of transplanting it to the circumstances of the Church to-day. In degree, exactly the same phenomenon has been occurring in the Roman Catholic Church in France, and also in the different Churches of Germany, Switzerland and elsewhere. Behind the Iron Curtain Christians mostly do their work in cells. They cannot help it. In fact, it is clear beyond all doubt that one of the instructions which the Holy Spirit has been giving to the twentieth-century Christendom is, " Give more and more of your time to Christian work in and among small groups of people, and establish the Household Church wherever you can."

Of all this movement S.C.K. is one part, and here, too, it has its own particular function and responsibility. Within the Cell Movement as a whole it stands for two necessary things. The first is mutual and self-imposed discipline. Half a dozen different and separate people will never really become a unity of heart and mind until they are obedient to each other. In S.C.K. this mutual obedience is provided for and made possible by a rule of life unanimously accepted, which always includes regular prayer for each other, and the regarding of the meetings of the company as a sacred obligation. It does not matter how simple a rule of life may be, but it is essential that there should be one. No cell of any kind will hold together without one, and no S.C.K. company is allowed to exist at all unless it has one.

The second feature of S.C.K. considered as part of the Cell Movement as a whole is still more important. It is the fact that there is enough—and only enough—organization to hold all the companies together, to keep track of them all, and to ensure that each one gets what help it needs and when it needs it. It is a very serious weakness of the rest of the Cell Movement that this provision so seldom appears to have been made. Nobody knows how many Christian cells there are, or where they are, or anything about them. This is no doubt because it is nobody's precise business to know.

But this is unfortunate because all experience shows that small groups of Christians reproduce corporately exactly the same needs and weaknesses as their individual members. They get weary and disheartened. They are tempted to give up because success is so long in coming to them. They need many kinds of help and do not know where to turn for it. They may luxuriate in their own sense of fellowship, turn their gaze inward upon themselves, and rest content in the contemplation of their own excellence. All these traps and more besides lie in their path. The only guard against them is what S.C.K. has from the first provided—an organization sufficient to hold all the companies together by a score of devices making it impossible for any company to live in isolation from all the others, and a system by which each one of them is regularly visited by somebody from the centre of the whole movement.

So, at last, this narrative has traced in outline ten years of history and has now reached the present day. The foundations of S.C.K. seem to be sound. The principles of Christian discipleship for which it stands can every one of them be verified in the Holy Scriptures themselves. Their working out in actual practice has been chequered and fumbling. It was bound to be so. To be faithful to the principles expressed in waiting upon God inevitably involved the necessity of groping for every step we took. Thus there has been a good deal of mire and clay to stumble through, and " success " and "failure"—impostors both—have been fairly evenly matched. These heats and pains were part of the process of growing up, and this narrative has not concealed them. As long as this was our state the rule of No

Publicity was plainly right, and it is the history of a hidden and largely unknown experiment that I have been writing.

But now, it seems to us all, we are growing up; and we know sufficient of this instrument to be sure about it. It offers, we are certain, a vital part of the answer to the situation which all Christians agree in deploring. Here is one contribution to the making of the key to unlock the door through which the whole Church must pass before this can again become a fully Christian country. Therefore we have thought it right to speak plainly and openly about it. What has been described does actually exist, though still in miniature, and is here to be used. We now offer it humbly to the Church, the mother of us all.